CONTENTS

THE
SAVAGE
STONE AGE

TERRY DEARY

Illustrated by
Martin Brown

To Erica Sheppard, with thanks

Scholastic Children's Books,
Commonwealth House, 1–19 New Oxford Street,
London WC1A 1NU, UK

A divsion of Scholastic Ltd
London ~ New York ~ Toronto ~ Sydney ~Auckland
Mexico City ~ New Delhi ~ Hong Kong

Published in the UK by Scholastic Ltd, 1999

Text copyright © Terry Deary, 1999
Illustrations copyright © Martin Brown, 1999

ISBN 0 590 65889 1

All rights reserved
Typeset by M Rules
Printed and bound by Cox & Wyman Ltd, Reading, Berks.

10

The right of Terry Deary and Martin Brown to be identified as the author and illustrator of this work respectively has been asserted by them in accordance with the Copyright, Designs and Patents Act, 1988.

INTRODUCTION

History can be horrible. And the further back in time you go, the more horrible it becomes in some ways! Of course not everyone believes this! Some people would quite like the idea of time travel. They'd like to go back in time and live in another age. An age without homework, global warming and mad cow disease.

I'D LIKE TO LIVE A COUPLE OF HUNDRED YEARS AGO! NO TEACHERS! NO POLICEMEN! AND NO BRUSSELS SPROUTS!

INSTEAD YOU COULD BE HANGED FOR STEALING A SHEEP, BE KNEE-DEEP IN HORSE DROPPINGS IN THE STREET AND HAVE NO SOFT TOILET PAPER!

WHAT? NO SOFT TOILET PAPER?

So the past isn't so attractive as it seems in the school books.

BUT GO BACK OVER A THOUSAND YEARS AND YOU HAD NO BORING SHOPPING, NO DRUNKEN DRIVERS TO KNOCK YOU OFF YOUR BIKE - NO BIKE!

AND A THOUSAND YEARS AGO YOU HAD THE WORRY OF STARVING FROM A BAD HARVEST, BEING MURDERED BY VIKING INVADERS OR DYING FROM A ROTTEN TOOTH

Still, some people think the past was a time when life was simple and easy. A million years ago you had no books (not even *Horrible Histories* because there was no history), no hot, soapy baths to get rid of the lice on your body and no smelly socks!

But would you like to find out what the Stone Age was really like to live in? You could go to a museum and see flint arrowheads in glass cases or poor paintings of hairy people in animal skins. But that doesn't tell you how people *lived* ... and *died*.

You may decide to climb into your time machine, set the dial to 1 million years BC, and switch on.[1]

If you can't manage a time machine then what you need is a book that will tell you the truth about the savagery of the Stone Age. What you need is a horrible history of 'prehistoric' people – people who existed in those happy times before 'history' was invented. Strange as it may seem ... stranger even than time travel ... you have the very book in your hands at this moment.

So what are you waiting for? The next Stone Age?

1. To get instructions on how to make a time machine you need to wait until the year AD 2346 when the first one will be invented. If you can't wait that long then you will need an alarm clock, a wire coat hanger, a banana and a copy of tomorrow's newspaper – *The Times*, of course.

STONE AGE TIMELINE

3,500,000 years ago (y.a.) Footprints have been found in east Africa that are over three-and-a-half million years old. They show that creatures we call 'hominids' can walk on two legs. Big deal, you say! Even a baby in nappies can do that! Yes, but this allows the front feet to develop into hands and to use tools.[1] These 'hominids' will take over the world, you'll see.

3,200,000 y.a. Skeleton has been found in Africa of 'Lucy', who walked on two legs. She was nicknamed after the Beatles song *Lucy in the Sky with Diamonds*! She's only four feet tall and her brain is just 400 cc big.[2] Archaeologists have found evidence that a family of nine similar hominids were killed in a sudden disaster – maybe they were too pea-brained to run away! This is the first ever horrible human history event we know about.

2,500,000 y.a. Earliest stone tools found in Ethiopia show

1. The posh name for these hominids is 'Australopithecus' which means 'southern apes' and not to be confused with 'Australians' – who are also southern apes except for Martin Brown who is wonderful.
2. Modern humans have a brain of around 1,550 cc. Take yours out and measure it. If it's as small as Lucy's then you will probably make a good teacher.

these hominids knew how to scrape the skin off their food ... but that didn't mean they had weapons to kill it. So experts think they probably stole dead meat from wild animals. (Drop some sweets on the classroom floor and see that many of today's hominids still have this dirty, thieving habit!)

2,500,000–1,500,000 y.a. Early hominids are changing into more 'modern' human beings and are using stone tools. They are called 'handy humans' (*Homo habilis* is the posh scientific name).

1,800,000 y.a. The clever humans build their first houses – in Tanzania – a half-circle of lava blocks probably covered with branches. Not too comfortable but at least there's no rent to pay, no poll tax and your neighbours don't park their BMW next door to make you jealous.

1,790,000 y.a. Another type of Australopithecine is living in Kenya. That's a bit of a mouthful to say – and as he had a bit of a mouthful of big crunching teeth he gets the name 'Nutcracker Man'. The archaeologists who

found him thought his teeth were strong enough to crack nuts. (Not to be confused with your local football hooligan who is 'Nutcaser man'.)

1,600,000 y.a. Hominids have grown larger than 'Nutcracker' and are using cleverer tools. These 'upright humans' (*Homo erectus* if you want to be posh) are spreading from Africa. But archaeologists have also found 'handy humans' who were still living at this time. The finders gave them more cheerful nicknames like 'Twiggy', 'George' and 'Cinderella'. (Not to be confused with your school goalie whose nickname is 'Cinderella' because he's always late for the ball.)

1,000,000 y.a. Possibly the first use of fire. And now there's another new type of hominid – the one that will become *you* in a million years' time: 'wise man' (or *Homo sapiens)*, who has a bigger brain (1,400 cc as opposed to 840–1,066 cc of *erectus*). There are other types of hominid around at this time, but *Homo sapiens* is the only one that will become your ancestor. In June

1998 a skull was found in Eritrea in north-east Africa belonging to the oldest *Homo sapiens* ever found – before this, most people thought *Homo sapiens* first appeared 450,000 years ago. This is the start of what historians will call the Old Stone Age – 'Palaeolithic', if you want a gold star.

800,000 y.a. Hominids arrive in Europe, probably because that's where the best food is. (No, the animals, berries and fruit – not the pizzerias, which haven't been invented yet.)

500,000 y.a. *Homo erectus* strolls into Europe.

450,000 y.a. *Homo sapiens* is spreading around the world and eating cooked food. Not that you'd want to share some of it!

200,000–130,000 y.a. Neanderthals appear in Europe. These are not *Homo sapiens* but hominids that are almost as clever. Trouble is they are not clever enough to survive and will end up extinct.

150,000 y.a. European humans in the Ice Age start to use caves to shelter from the cold. One tricky problem is that bears like them too, and there must have been a

few bedroom battles for the cosiest caves!

128,000 y.a. Sea levels rise as Ice Age ends. Britain is cut off from Europe and in the warmer weather there are hippos in the Thames. They're not there now so there's no point looking. But did some prehistoric creatures survive in deep lakes like Loch Ness?

120,000–100,000 y.a. *Homo sapiens* are becoming 'near-modern' humans – *Homo sapiens sapiens* or wise-wise human – and these clever clogs are living in Africa. You wouldn't be too shocked to see one of these in your classroom – if it had shaved and washed and dressed, of course. Those Neanderthals seem to be top hominids in Europe.

70,000–30,000 y.a. Colder again, new Ice Age and *Homo sapiens sapiens* moves into Europe. Early humans discover Australia and move in: this is bad news for kangaroos. In Europe and Asia hominids are burying their dead – men are buried with meat and tools, women with nothing.

40,000 y.a. Hominids are getting really clever at making tools. It's

11

becoming the first 'industry'. They are also creating art. Small sculptures and paintings. The ones that they are scratching and painting in caves will survive until today.

30,000 y.a. Neanderthals still present in Spain but about to disappear without trace, leaving just *Homo sapiens sapiens* to take over the world. Probably the first hominids arrive in America. Bad news for bison.

25,000–14,000 y.a. The Ice Age returns for the last time. Maybe the Neanderthals saw it coming and decided to become extinct rather than live through another 10,000 freezing years.

15,000 y.a. Super-humans from space built ancient monuments. Their civilization is now buried beneath Antarctic. No, that's not in your school history books, but some seriously potty people believe it. Make up your own mind. (Unless you're one of the seriously potty people in which case you haven't got a mind and can't make it up.)

12,000–10,000 BC End of last Ice Age and start of what is known as

the Middle Stone Age – Mesolithic period. Humans are making pottery and building mud-brick houses. In America, beavers the size of donkeys are hunted down till they are extinct. Just as well. Imagine one of them chewing at your telegraph poles.

8,500–7,300 BC Humans are farming cereal grasses for the first time. Dug-out canoes are being used. People settling and gathering into towns. Jericho has a population of 2,000 people.

7,000 BC Copper is being used in Turkey and Iran.

5,000 BC Bronze used widely but these times are still known as the Stone Age.

4,000 BC Start of what historians call the New Stone Age – the 'Neolithic' period.

3,200 BC Sumerian people of Mesopotamia invent writing. Now they can write horrible history, so that's the end of prehistory. Exciting things like spelling tests are now possible.

3,000 BC The earliest part of First Stonehenge is built. Archaeologists can't agree why it was built. Horrible historians

suspect they may be world's first football goal-posts.

2,000 BC Bronze is now being used by many humans, so this becomes known as the start of the Bronze Age. It's goodbye to the Stone Age … except in places where bronze isn't being used where it is still the Stone Age.

700–500 BC Early Iron Age, so now you can iron your clothes.

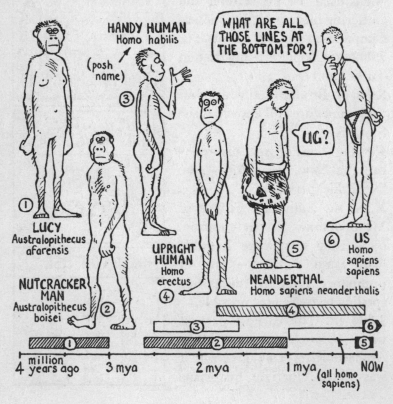

14

AWFUL FOR ANIMALS

Have you ever crunched on North American camel flavoured crisps? No.

Ever munched on mammoth mince? No.

Ever popped Kentucky Fried moa in your mouth? Noa![1]

Because they no longer exist.

All these ancient animals had lived happily on Earth for a million or more years till the hungry hominids came along. Now they're all dead, deceased, demised, defunct, defeated, discontinued, departed, dustbinned and done-for daisy-pushers.

Extinct ... or, in the case of the moa, egg-stinct.

Where have they gone? Cruelly killed by heartless hominids.

1. Moas were flightless birds that lived in New Zealand – till humans arrived and had moa massacres. They could be up to three metres tall. They'd never seen humans before so they were easy to catch and kill. A few survived till about 200 years ago.

Horrible hunters

Early hominids pinched corpses from killer animals like lions and ate the scraps. They made stone tools to scrape the meat off the skin and eat it raw. (You can try this the next time your cat brings a half-eaten mouse into the house.) Then some clever hominids discovered something important...

Stone tools became stone weapons. By 700,000 years ago a new type of Stone Age tool, the hand axe, was being used. 250,000 years ago the humans had wooden spears with tips hardened in fire. By 9,000 BC the horrible humans had invented bows and arrows.

Animals used to run away to save themselves, but now the new weapons, and the human brain behind them, drove those animals to destruction.

But how *do* you kill a mighty mammoth or catch a herd of horses when you only have stone weapons? Use your 1,550 cc brain. Stone Age people did!

As early as 300,000 years ago hunters in Spain stampeded elephants into swamps and butchered them. Stone Age people seem simple to us, yet an elephant hunt took a lot of organizing. (You couldn't do it if you tried! But *don't* try it because elephants are a protected species. Hunt traffic wardens instead – they are not a protected species.)

In 18,000 BC horse hunters in France used a natural cliff as a fall-trap.

In America (about 10,000 years ago) they stampeded bison over cliffs. Bison were hunted because the American camels and mammoths had been wiped out.

Hunters – run and chase

Bison – break necks

Cliff – big drop

Brave warrior underneath cliff to finish off

Warning: Don't get too brave and try to catch bison as they land

American Plains Indians had a bison hunt once a year, in autumn, so they'd have meat for the winter.

The Plains Indians arranged lines of stones into a funnel that led to the cliff and stampeded the bison between the stones. One mistake could scatter the whole herd and the tribe could starve to death over the winter.

These were clever hominids and not simple, hairless apes. Can you say the same about your classmates?

Toasted tortoise

Native American Indians in Florida, 14,000 years before Disney World, hunted an extinct type of giant tortoise. (Well, it wasn't extinct when they hunted it, of course, but it's extinct now. That's what you get if you can't run away fast enough.)

Archaeologists found one of these tortoises with a sharp

wooden stake driven through it. This would kill the creature and then be useful for holding it over a fire to roast.

This could be proof of the world's oldest barbecue!

These Florida food-lovers also ate rattlesnakes and hairy elephants called mastodons. Slow-moving tree-loving sloths must have been easy to catch and kill.

A dog's life

Not all animals suffered at the hands of Stone Agers. A graveyard has been found in Sweden that contains a doggy cemetery.

The dogs were buried with the same sort of grave goods that their human owners had – deer antlers, axes and flint blades (to open the tins of dog-food in the afterlife?).

If they were that respected after death then it's a fair guess they were well treated in their doggy lives – better than many dogs are today – because they were such a help in hunting.

19

FOUL FOOD

Stone Age humans couldn't pop down to their local supermarket and then shove food into their microwave ovens. Everything they ate had to be found or caught. If they wanted it cooked then they had to do it themselves.

By studying hunter-gatherer people who are alive today, historians have come up with a rough idea of how early Stone Age people brewed up breakfast, lapped up lunch, tucked into tea or scoffed their supper.

Dreadful dinners

Tasty tips for hungry house-husbands and weary wives

You will need:
- x dead animals - enough to feed the family
- x a stone knife
- x a flint to strike a light and wood for a fire

Methods:
1. Catch a bird or animal. (Handy hint: hang around beasts of prey like lions. Wait till they've eaten their fill and take what's left - but make sure they don't make a snack of you!)
2. Light the fire and build it up to a good blaze. (Handy hint: once you've got a fire going it is a good idea to try and keep it going until you need it again.)

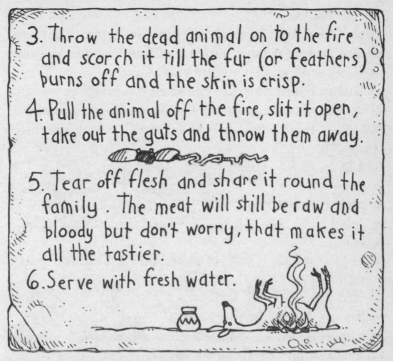

3. Throw the dead animal on to the fire and scorch it till the fur (or feathers) burns off and the skin is crisp.

4. Pull the animal off the fire, slit it open, take out the guts and throw them away.

5. Tear off flesh and share it round the family. The meat will still be raw and bloody but don't worry, that makes it all the tastier.

6. Serve with fresh water.

You may like to have a Stone Age dinner in the school canteen! Dinner ladies could prepare the food in Stone Age fashion and you can try to spot the difference.

And don't forget your manners…

Early Stone Age Table Manners

Clever cooks

Later Stone Age eaters weren't nearly as crude. They used spoons made of pottery, horn or wood and would cook stews or joints of meat in boiling water.

You may think Stone-Agers weren't as bright as you. But could you solve the problem of cooking without a metal pot?

The riddle
You have:

- straw
- plaited straw ropes
- wood
- stones
- a stone trough – slabs of stone joined to make a water-tight box
- cold water
- fire
- a leg of lamb

... and a hungry family, of course.

Well? Have you worked it out? Or are you too dumb to be a Stone-Ager?

Here's what they'd do...

The Sunday Stone Age Cookery Page

Is your family tired of the same old raw eggs for Sunday lunch? Try this exciting recipe from our super chef!

1 Light the fire near the trough.
2 Put the stones in the fire.
3 Fill the trough with water.

4 Wrap the meat in a bundle of straw and tie the ends with straw ropes.

5 When the stones are red hot lift them from the fire with pieces of wood.

6 Drop the stones into the water till it begins to boil.

7 Lower the straw-wrapped meat into the boiling water using the straw ropes.

8 Keep adding hot stones to keep the water boiling.

9 Lift the meat out after a couple of hours.

10 Unwrap the meat and eat it!

The straw wrapping not only made it easy to handle the meat, it also meant the meat didn't taste of ash from the hot stones.

They could also roast the meat by starting a fire in the trough to heat the stone, dropping in the meat and covering it with hot stones. Or they might barbecue it on a wooden spit over an open fire – the trouble was the wooden spit could catch fire and dump the meat in the fire if they weren't careful. And it could end up black and charred on the outside and raw on the inside ... a bit like your dad's barbecued sausages.

Did you work out how to cook cave-style? If you did then you'd make a good Boy Scout or Girl Guide. Award yourself a Prehistoric Cookery badge!

Tasty treats

Stone-Agers had to work hard to get their food, so they didn't waste it. They'd eat things that you might not have tried...

- cow's udder (makes you shudder)
- blood (tastes good)
- feet (nice treat)
- brain (keeps you sane)
- lungs and tongues.

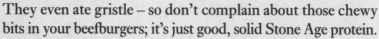

They even ate gristle – so don't complain about those chewy bits in your beefburgers; it's just good, solid Stone Age protein.

Some archaeologists think the Stone-Agers caught animals, slit open their stomachs and ate the meal that the animal had swallowed just before it was killed.

Yeuch! Remember that and you'll never complain about your mother's cooking ever again!

The bones in caves and graves tell scientists what animals Stone-Agers ate. Of course you can't cook many of them today because they're extinct (like the giant kangaroos of Australia) or they're now very rare – you don't get so many rhinos in Rotherham, elephants in Edinburgh or bears in Bournemouth as you did in the Ice Age. So you'll never know the joy of raw rhino or barbecued bear (unless you capture and cook a cute little koala).

But if you eat roast lamb or beef or chicken, then you'll be enjoying the same sort of taste as your ancient ancestors.

Shells and fish bones tell us what sort of seafood they ate – but they probably didn't invent the ancient joke ...

Scientists can tell what plants humans ate by looking under the microscope at Stone Age poo. (The posh word for ancient poo is 'coprolite' – you have to soak it for three days before examining it. Just thought you might like to know that.)

Try making this Stone Age treat known today as 'frumenty'. Experimental archaeologists examined the stomach of an Iron Age body and made this porridge using the recipe. They got volunteers to sample it and, of course, they lived!

You may enjoy it. You may prefer to stick with cornflakes. If you were a Stone-Ager you wouldn't have a lot of choice.

How did Stone-Agers discover cooking methods like this? Over thousands of years a lot of Stone-Agers must have eaten a lot of horrible things before they discovered what was safe and tasty.

Your mushroom omelette is safe because thousands of Stone-Agers must have died eating deadly toadstools.

Did you know…?

Archaeologists used coprolites to study the sort of food Stone-Agers ate. But they could also use them to discover what sort of worms and parasites prehistoric people carried around in their guts! And you thought archaeology was a glamorous sort of job?

GROOVY GAMES

Human beings enjoy a good laugh. They are the only creatures that *do* laugh. So Stone-Agers must have chuckled as they chatted and guffawed over goofy games we can only guess at.

It wasn't all work and hunting. Some scientists reckon that Stone-Agers spent as little as 15 to 19 hours a week working to survive. That's even less than your teachers (though Stone-Agers didn't get the long summer holidays, of course).

What did Stone-Agers do in their leisure time?

Did they, for example, have competitions to see who could suck the brains from a skull the fastest? Did they spin a stone scraper and play Postman's Rock? Did they poke someone's eyes out with a stone spear and play Blind Man's Bluff? Who knows?

The few clues we have give us some ideas...

Follow my leader

Want to play a simple game that amused a young person three-and-a-half million years ago?

It all began in 1978 (which isn't three-and-a-half million years ago – be patient!) when a group of young scientists were working at an archaeology dig in Africa. They were having a little game of their own, which involved throwing lumps of elephant poo at one another.

WHAP!

One of these scientists ducked a lump of flying elephant dung, slipped and fell flat on his face.

WHOP

What did he find under his nose? No, not elephant dung. Some curious dents in the rock. Dents that looked remarkably like footsteps.

When the area was cleared the scientists found two sets of footsteps, side by side. They had been printed into volcano ash that had set hard 3.7 million years ago. When they looked really closely they saw that the larger footprints (Dad's perhaps) had smaller footprints inside.

We can guess that a child had followed its parents and amused itself by stepping in father's footsteps.

Next time you're on a beach with your parents you can try it – and experience something nearly four million years old.

(You may prefer to try the game of throwing elephant poo at your friends. Of course you'll have to wait till an elephant happens to wander down your street. It has never been known to work with doggy droppings … so don't try it.)

Wedding wisdom

For this fortune-telling game you need to go to Dundalk in Ireland. You'll find a prehistoric tomb there made of three pillars about two metres high with a 30-tonne slab of rock on top.

You'll notice that the rock slopes.

Pick up a pebble and throw it on to the roof.

If the pebble rolls off you are safe, but if the pebble stays on the roof, then you'll be married within a year!

This probably won't work if you throw stones at the roof of your house – so don't try it.

This is a modern custom but the belief in the power of the stones may go back into prehistory.

Power painting

You need:

- the bone from a fillet of lamb (ask your butcher – or use the bone from a leg of lettuce if you're a vegetarian)
- poster paint
- a cave wall (if you haven't a handy cave then use any blank wall/teacher's car/ Dad's-best-white-shirt-on-the-washing-line)
- running shoes

Method:

1 Boil the bone and scrape the marrow from the inside so you have a tube.

2 Dip the end of the tube in the paint and suck gently – but don't suck the paint into your mouth!

3 Place your hand against the cave wall/blank wall/teacher's car/Dad's-best-white-shirt-on-the-washing-line.

4 Take aim with the bone-tube at your hand and blow.

5 The paint will spray your hand and leave the outline on the cave wall.

6 If you've used a classroom wall/teacher's car/Dad's-best-shirt-on-the-washing-line, then have the running shoes handy for a fast getaway.

Sometimes the painters used reeds rather than bones to blow through. If you are really idle/boring/stupid, you can use a straw as a spray tube.

Note: Some experts don't believe that Stone-Agers spray-painted in this way.

Other methods:
Sometimes the artists picked up a lump of coloured iron mineral rock and used it as a crayon. But painting was most common. They used hair from the animals they'd killed to make brushes.

You could take a lolly stick and chew one end till it is frayed. Dip it in poster paint and use the frayed stick as a brush. This makes painting difficult but at least you'll see how clever the cave artists were to work like that.

They added delicious details to the paintings – so a bison may be shown on its back, dead, with its guts spilling out.

Some archaeologists believe this was meant to be helpful magic – if they painted a deer/mammoth/bison killed by hunters, then next day the painting, like a dream, would come truc. The painting made sure the hunt would be a success.

Or maybe the cave artists simply enjoyed painting. Some people do.

You could paint a passing mammoth yourself. (If you can't find a mammoth then paint a cat.)

For light, the cave workers used dishes filled with animal fats and a reed wick. But an electric light is easier and doesn't smell half as bad.

BATTY BELIEFS

It's impossible to know when Stone-Agers started believing in a life after death or in some sort of religion. But it's a fair guess that it happened around the time they started burying people carefully in graves with their precious objects. The oldest known grave (near Nazareth in the Middle East) is 100,000 years old.

Many Stone-Agers continued to dump their dead in the family rubbish heap where passing dogs would munch them for lunch. Historians have learned a lot from the graves where bodies were laid properly to rest and covered to protect them from becoming a sabre-toothed tiger's tea.

Grave test

Here are ten things that Stone-Agers were buried with over the centuries ... can you spot which one is *false*?

1 Teeth that had fallen out in life
2 A hacked-off arm
3 A dead baby
4 Ropes to tie the arms and legs
5 A necklace of animal teeth
6 A live cat
7 Sea shells
8 Food
9 Flowers
10 A dead dog

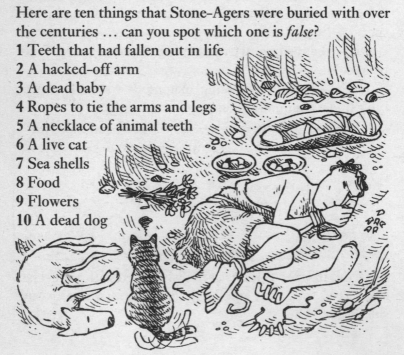

Answers: All are true except **6**.

1 In Yorkshire an old woman was buried with all the teeth she'd lost during her life. Stone-Agers had no money so the tooth fairy had nothing to trade, I guess. The teeth had been tucked neatly under her chin. Did the dead woman's friends think she'd need them in the next life, perhaps?

2 Not far away from her a man was buried with his arm that had been cut off in some sort of fight. The chopped-off arm was placed on his shoulder with the fingertips touching his face. Weird, eh?

3 A third grave showed the cremated bones of a child, packed in clay and buried with an adult. Did the adult die first and was the child sacrificed and burned to keep the corpse company? The world's oldest burial at Nazareth also shows a six-year-old child buried at the feet of an adult. Some children have been found buried in their parent's arms. Sweet.

4 The ropes that tied up a Stone Age burial may have been an attempt to stop the corpse jumping out of the grave and haunting the family…

5 …And their 'jewellery' made sure they looked smart as they wandered around the afterlife.

7 In the Cheddar Gorge (England) a young man was found buried with a necklace of sea-shells. These must have been collected 30 miles away so his people travelled widely even though bicycles hadn't been invented! The Cheddar man had been buried after much of his flesh had rotted away. Nice job for some Stone Age undertaker.

8 In 1823 a skeleton called 'The Red Lady of Paviland' was found in Wales by a professor called William Buckland. He said it was a Roman who'd been buried along with the bones of animals that drowned in Noah's flood. In fact, the 'Roman' Red 'Lady' turned out to be a *prehistoric* 25-year-old *man* and the animal bones belonged to a mammoth. Young Mister Red Lady was buried with a handful of periwinkles (who hadn't drowned in Noah's flood).

A Polish Stone-Ager was buried with joints of wild-cat and beaver, *and* with his bow and arrows so he could catch more when he'd scoffed the cat (curried no doubt) and the beaver (boiled, perhaps). He was also buried sitting up so it was easier to hunt!

'BOUT THE ONLY THING I'M GOING TO HUNT DOWN HERE IS A MOLE

9 Flowers are placed on graves today and it seems they were used by Neanderthals too. Seven different types of flower were found in one bunch on the Turkish border. There was also a butterfly buried along with the bunch, probably by accident.

SNIFF

WILT

10 In Hungary an old man was buried with a dog. It must have been his pet when he was alive and it was killed to keep him company in the next life.

Did you know…?

Talking of grave tests, Lord Bath had some prehistoric bones taken from Cheddar Gorge (where the necklace of sea-shells was found). He had them tested to see if they were his relatives.

This sort of thing is important to aristocrats – King James I of England said he could trace his ancestors back to Noah! Lord Bath wanted to trace his ancestors back to the Stone Age.

His lordship was disappointed. The nearest living relative to the bones wasn't Lord Bath. It was his butler!

TEST YOUR TEACHER

Your teacher may *look* like a prehistoric Neanderthal but you can be pretty sure s/he *isn't*. Neanderthals are extinct, sadly, and teachers aren't ... sadly.

TEACHER   NEANDERTHAL

So you can test their 1,550 cc brains with this cruelly cunning cwiz and be pretty sure they aren't answering from memory.

Or test yourself. Score eight to ten and you are probably human. Four to seven and you are Neanderthal. Score one to three and you are a chimpanzee. Score nothing and you probably need to evolve for a few thousand years more.

1 Archaeologists could tell what prehistoric Egyptians were eating 11,000 years before the pyramids were built. What did they study?
a) Egyptian cookery books drawn on rocks and buried beneath the sand
b) ancient baby poo
c) ancient jawbones with food stuck between the teeth because toothbrushes hadn't been invented

2 Stone-Agers made their own paint from iron minerals coloured yellow, red, brown or black. These powder paints had to be mixed with a liquid before they could be painted on the cave walls. What liquid?

a) mammoth's pee
b) gooseberry beer
c) blood

3 What did Stone-Agers use instead of toilet paper?

a) moss
b) deer skin
c) hedgehog skin

4 In 1915, Stonehenge monument was put up for auction. Who bought it and why?

a) a fairground owner, who planned to use it as the centre of a Stone Age theme park – 'Caveworld'

b) an American who planned to put it on display in California
c) a rich man, as a present for his wife

5 How did Bolivian Stone-Agers keep their potatoes fresh

where they lived high in the Andes mountains?
a) by burying them in a potato pit
b) by frying them in llama fat till they had crisps and sealing them in little llama-leather packets
c) by freezing them

6 The fossil tooth of an ancient Chinese hominid was found where?
a) when builders were putting up the great wall of China
b) in a Chinese chemist shop
c) in a Chinese take-away restaurant

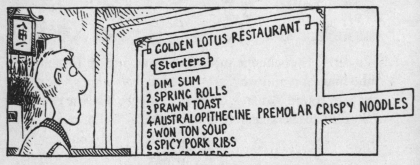

7 What did some clean Stone-Agers do that even modern humans forget?
a) cleaned their teeth
b) polished their shoes
c) washed up after dinner

8 Who had the first boomerangs?
a) Stone Age Australians
b) Stone Age North American Indians
c) modern Australians in 1822

9 How did Stone-Agers celebrate great occasions?
a) by setting off fireworks

b) by drinking lots of booze

c) by wrestling with cave bears

10 How did Stone-Agers in Sweden help their dead into the afterlife?
a) scratched a map on a stone to show them the way
b) left the door to the tomb open so the spirit could get out
c) shot arrows into corpses as they lay in their graves

Answers:

1b) Most of the plants left behind by prehistoric Egyptians had rotted away. But some were preserved because they had been charred at a camp-fire. Other plants were eaten by babies and came out in their poo. The mucky little infants dropped their poo in the camp. Tidy adults swept the baby-poo into the fire where it was baked hard and preserved. All the archaeologists had to do was cut it open and examine it under a microscope.

You might like to try this in your house if you have a baby brother or sister! On the other hand, you may not.

2c) Don't try this in school. Mixing powder paints with blood *will* help them to flow over the walls and to last over 30,000 years. You could find your pictures are very attractive … to vampires. Stone Age artists may also have used animal fats to mix the paint. This was before the time when they learned how to use these fats to make chips.

3a) If you said 'hedgehog skin', then you deserve to try it! A Stone Age body found preserved in ice had lumps of moss in his woven-grass handbag and this moss was his toilet paper. You don't get this sort of fascinating fact in your  boring old school books, do you? And you've always wanted to know what Stone-Agers did before toilet paper was invented, haven't you?

4c) Cecil Chubb was having breakfast with his wife and mentioned that Stonehenge was being put up for auction that day. 'Ooooh! I'd love to own it!' his wife said. 'Then I'll put in an offer,' her adoring husband told her. His offer was accepted and it became Mrs Chubb's. If it had been her birthday, they could have stuck candles on the stones to celebrate. In 1918, Cecil and his wife decided to give the monument to the British government to look after – the Brit people got Stonehenge, Cecil got a knighthood.

5c) The Tiwanaku people of Bolivia lived so high in the Andes that the temperatures dropped to minus 20°C at night. The tricky Tiwanaku divided their farm fields into long narrow strips and surrounded them with water-filled ditches. The sun warmed the water during the day and the warmth kept the fields from freezing at night – like a hot-water bottle. That allowed them to grow more potatoes than they could eat at once, so they also invented a way of freezing them to eat in the winter months. They sprinkled the potatoes with water and left them out at night to freeze and be preserved.

6b) The tooth was found in a Chinese chemist shop in 1899. For centuries chemists in China had bought fossil teeth and ground them up to use in their medicines. The chemists believed they were dragon teeth with magic powers. It was thought to be an ancient human at the time but now many scientists think it came from an ape after all.

7a) The skeleton of a Palaeolithic young man, found in

England, showed that he had almost certainly cleaned his teeth regularly. Maybe he had a mum to nag him! 'Clean those teeth or the Palaeolithic dentist will get you with his stone drill!'

8b) In 12,000 BC Stone Age Indians in Florida used a boomerang.

Archaeologists reckon that the American boomerang *didn't* come back ... which, of course, spoils the joke!

9a) ... if you believe an Oxford Museum professor. He reckoned Stone-Agers made pottery figures about 25,000 years ago. At a religious ceremony they'd be thrown on to a fire and explode. The figures were soaked in water so they would take a little while to dry out before they went off – that would give the firework-thrower time to get safely away, like a modern firework that tells you to light the blue touch paper and retire!

10c) Swedes fired arrows into their corpses, though we don't know why. (This is better than corpses firing arrows into swedes which would be a real turnip for the book.) They buried their dead with loving care in graves in the earth and in log canoes under water. Firing arrows into a body can't have been an insult. It must have had some special meaning – maybe it punctured the skin and let the spirit out ... or maybe it was just easy target practice.

AWFUL ARCHAEOLOGISTS

Modern humans have been digging up ancient humans for hundreds of years and trying to work out the answer to the big question…

The diggers–up–of–the–past don't think being called 'diggers–up–of–the–past' is a posh enough name, so they call themselves *archaeologists*.

Ancient horrible historical joke 1:
The mystery writer Agatha Christie was married to an archaeologist and cracked the following joke…

An archaeologist is the best husband any woman can have: the older she gets, the more interested he is in her.

Don't blame me. I never said it was a *good* joke.

Ancient horrible historical joke 2:
An archaeologist's joke is no better…

Clearly some archaeologists have sad lives.

Battles over the birth of the Earth

The Bible says that God created the universe in six days, then had a kip on the seventh.

His last great creation was to take a lump of clay and make a man. Finally He breathed up the clay man's nostrils and brought him to life. (Yeuch! How would you like someone breathing up your nostrils?) The man was called Adam.

Early historians were interested in the actual date that God had blown up Adam's nose and risked a mouth full of snot. Perhaps every human on Earth could have a big birthday party on that day! Sadly, they couldn't agree on the year, never mind the day. The world began in...

Roman Catholics went back further. They said God made Earth in 5199 BC.

They were very annoyed when archaeologists tried to tell them they were wrong…

THERE WAS NO SUCH MAN AS ADAM, THE EARTH WAS HERE FOR MILLIONS OF YEARS BEFORE HUMANS AND WE EVOLVED FROM CREATURES LIKE MONKEYS

GASP!

In 1616 the Italian thinker Lucilio Vanini said that humans evolved from apes. Church leaders went ape at the idea, decided to teach him a lesson and had him burned alive.

The archaeologists produced stones that had been shaped by prehistoric humans – arrowheads, for example. Those who believed in the Bible had different explanations…

THESE ARE ACTUALLY THUNDERBOLTS MADE BY PASSING STORM CLOUDS

THESE ARE ROCKS SHAPED BY NATURE

THE TRUTH IS THEY ARE ARROWHEADS… FROM THE BOWS OF FAIRIES

Archaeologists showed these weapons had been found alongside creatures (like mammoths) that had been dead for hundreds of thousands of years. But until 1847 they didn't believe humans and mammoths lived on Earth at the same time. They did!

Even ancient dinosaur bones, millions of years old, could also be explained by the Bible believers…

These ancient bones were believed to have magical powers. They were set in gold rings and sold as lucky charms or ground into powder to make miraculous medicines.

When settlers from Europe saw Native American Indians using similar arrowheads they got the message. In 1699 Edward Lhwyd wrote…

These arrowheads were once used for shooting in Britain as they still are in America. Some foolish people say they have seen them drop out of the air, shot by fairies. I will believe that when I see it for myself.

FAIRY 'NUFF!

In the 1600s, some scientists put together a collection of prehistoric bones and came up with this image…

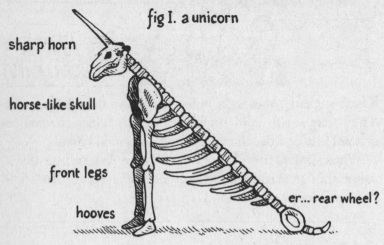

fig I. a unicorn

sharp horn

horse-like skull

front legs

hooves

er… rear wheel?

Until the late 1850s some scientists and historians still argued that the Earth was about 6,000 years old.

Not an Irish joke!
In 1857, a workman was digging in a cave in a quarry in the Neander Valley in Germany (*Neanderthal* in German). He found an old skeleton deep in the clay.

fig II.

His workmates were about to throw it away when the quarry manager rescued it. He took it to a local teacher to see if he knew what it was. The skull had a low forehead and thick ridges above the eyes. The teacher said, 'I recognize this!' (No, it wasn't from

~~thicko~~ *thick*
brow ridges

looking in the mirror!) 'Look at those thick ridges over the brows – just like a gorilla. This is an ancient type of human!' He was right, of course, but not many people believed him at first.

The disbelievers said, 'This is the skull of a modern human – but it's either an idiot ... or an Irishman!'

If these people thought the Irish were Stone-Agers then *they* were the idiots, not the Irish!

Nasty Neanderthals

During the Stone Age there were two main types of hominid – *Homo sapiens* (they were your ancestors), and Neanderthals, who had flat heads, a thick bony bulge over the eyes, short legs and some very nasty habits. You'll be pleased to know that Neanderthals died out, so you needn't have nightmares about being nobbled by a Neanderthal in the night.

The nasty Neanderthals seem to have been head-hunters. Here's the evidence...

- Neanderthal skulls have been found which show they were clubbed to death.
- The base of the skulls had been opened up to get the brains out ... to eat? Or so the killer could get the strength and wisdom from the victim's brain?

I'VE GOT MORE BRAINS THAN YOU

- Neanderthals dug two pits in the floor of a cave and packed them with skulls. The skulls had been hacked from the bodies, brought to the cave one at a time and packed in so they all faced the sunset.

- The 20 children and nine young women in these pits were buried with ornaments made of deer's teeth and snails' shells.

Just in case you think the head-hackers took the brain-boxes off bodies that had died naturally, consider this bit of evidence:

- At least five of the skulls' owners had been killed by hatchet blows to the head.

Neanderthals have been accused of being cannibals. The evidence for this is not so strong...

- Human bones have been found mixed with left-over food.

- Human bones have been smashed, perhaps to extract the tasty marrow inside.

- Human bones have been scorched by fire as if they were cooked.

Not exactly 'proof'. But if you meet someone with a flat head and short legs and they say...

… it may be wise to say, 'Thanks – but no thanks!' just to be on the safe side.

And it wasn't only humans who were sacrificed and beheaded. Twenty bears' skeletons were buried in a pit in France and in the Alps seven bears' skulls were stored in a stone chest. All of the bears' muzzles pointed towards the door. Weird, huh?

In Poland, the Neanderthals decorated their cave walls with bears' skulls while German Neanderthals kept a captive bear and filed its front teeth down to make it safer … not that it's safe trying to file a bear's teeth because it still has slashing claws. (Before you even consider doing this to a bear in your back garden … paws!)

Japanese Stone-Agers captured young bears, filed their teeth and later killed them in some sort of ceremony. 50,000 years later and humans still love their teddy bears. Nothing changes, does it?

Awesome archaeologists

In the 1800s archaeologists weren't scientists. Some were really curious about the past – like you are or you wouldn't be reading this book. But many were treasure hunters seeking lots of money and lots of glory. The money would be hidden gold and the glory would be in uncovering some great secrets of the past like...

- whatever happened to dinosaurs?
- was there really a Wooden Horse of Troy?
- who invented the wheel?

These great puzzles are still unsolved today. Though we can make some good guesses, can't we?

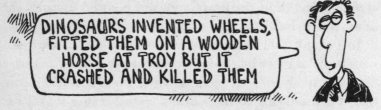

DINOSAURS INVENTED WHEELS, FITTED THEM ON A WOODEN HORSE AT TROY BUT IT CRASHED AND KILLED THEM

Victorian archaeologists were a bit like Indiana Jones ... fighting their way through dangers to uncover treasures from the past. They were also a bit like Attila the Hun – leading armies into other lands to pinch their wealth.

HAVE YOU GOT AN ARMY I COULD BORROW? THE HILL TRIBES HAVE A LOVELY BIG STATUE THAT WOULD LOOK RATHER NICE IN MY MUSEUM BUT THE CHEEKY LITTLE BLIGHTERS WON'T GIVE IT TO ME

Sir Austen Henry Layard (1817–1894) led armies of workers into Iraq, tunnelled into ancient palaces and packed the greatest finds off to Britain. (They can still be seen in the British Museum, which refuses to give them back to the countries they were stolen from.)

It wasn't only the British who robbed ancient sites, of course. In some countries it was a full-time job!

Piecing together the past

Archaeologists who investigated the Stone Age weren't so popular. After all, they didn't bring home treasure. And it was hard work! Take this simple story from an archaeologist's notebook, for example…

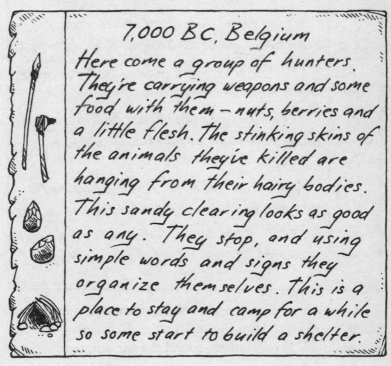

7,000 BC, Belgium

Here come a group of hunters. They're carrying weapons and some food with them – nuts, berries and a little flesh. The stinking skins of the animals they've killed are hanging from their hairy bodies. This sandy clearing looks as good as any. They stop, and using simple words and signs they organize themselves. This is a place to stay and camp for a while so some start to build a shelter.

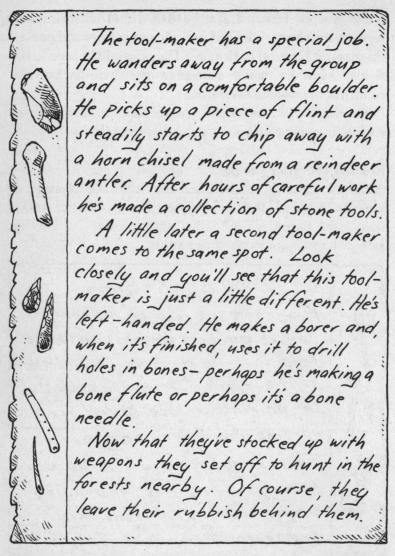

The tool-maker has a special job. He wanders away from the group and sits on a comfortable boulder. He picks up a piece of flint and steadily starts to chip away with a horn chisel made from a reindeer antler. After hours of careful work he's made a collection of stone tools.

A little later a second tool-maker comes to the same spot. Look closely and you'll see that this tool-maker is just a little different. He's left-handed. He makes a borer and, when it's finished, uses it to drill holes in bones — perhaps he's making a bone flute or perhaps it's a bone needle.

Now that they've stocked up with weapons they set off to hunt in the forests nearby. Of course, they leave their rubbish behind them.

We know that story is mostly *true*, even though it happened 9,000 years ago. How do we know? Because a Belgian archaeologist, David Cahen, found the site and...

- Marked the position of every fragment of stone.
- Put all the fragments back together again like a 3-D jigsaw puzzle.
- Examined the borer under a microscope and saw where it had been worn by the bone.

This took him *months*! He even saw that one of the borers had been used anticlockwise and worked out that the toolmaker had been left-handed!

Want to be an archaeologist of the Stone Age?

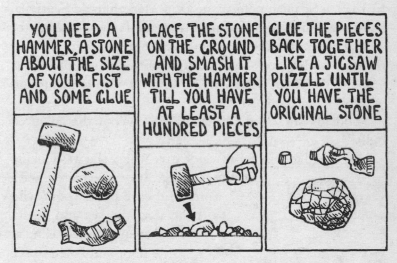

It shouldn't take you much more than a month. Do you *still* want to be an archaeologist?

Quick question:

Archaeological accidents

You may think those old archaeologists knew what they were doing when they set out to dig for ancient evidence. But some searched for years and found very little – others found amazing new things by accident.

If you want to be an archaeologist then try some of these unusual methods:

1 Take your daughter digging

In 1859, a Spanish nobleman, Don Marcelino de Sautuola, had been searching a cave on his estate. He was looking for animal bones and flint tools, so where else would he look but the floor of the cave? After a couple of weeks he took his 12-year-old daughter, Maria, with him. She wandered around with his lantern, exploring.

Suddenly she cried, 'Papa! Papa! Look at the coloured bulls!'

He rushed to join her in a side cave where she was looking at the ceiling. It was covered with wonderful cave paintings of wild boar, deer, horses and bison. He'd spent weeks looking at the floor and failed to see the art on the roof of the ceiling.

At first no one believed these were paintings done by cave-dwellers. They said they'd been done by the Don. (And, let's face it, his story of failing to see the paintings is a bit odd.) It was over 30 years before more cave art was found, in France, and he was finally believed by everyone. The trouble is the Don had died by then. He died knowing everyone was calling him a liar.

The professors said 'Sorry' to Maria instead.

2 Hound hunting

During the Second World War four teenage boys were hunting in woods in France. The loutish lads were tracking a wounded bird with their dog. Suddenly the dog vanished into a hole at the foot of a cliff face. The boys crawled in to explore and discovered a hole in the ground that the dog had fallen into. They dropped stones and discovered the hole wasn't too deep. (Some stones would have fallen on the hound's head, wouldn't they?) They climbed down and rescued the dog.

The hole was the entrance to a cave and they had discovered one of the greatest cave-art displays of all time – the Lascaux caves. There were 1,500 engravings and 600 paintings, including bulls five metres long – imagine the sausages you could make from a bull like that!

The boys kept their secret for a week and returned with bicycle lamps to explore further before they told the local teacher, Leon Laval. He didn't believe their story at first!

What a distrustful teacher!

The caves were finally examined by experts who said the paintings were 17,000 years old. Well done, lads!

Visitors flocked in. They carried with them germs that formed a green mould all over the ancient artwork. Paintings that had survived 17,000 years were in danger of vanishing in 17! They were closed and sealed.

But ... there are rumours that the boys' hunting tale was a lie. One story says they were looking for a cave that an old woman had told them about. Why lie about it?

One possible explanation is that the boys didn't want to share the 'prize' with an old woman. And the prize was that the boys got comfortable jobs guiding visitors through the caves ... while the teacher got the best job of all. He was put in charge!

3 Catch butterflies

Olduvai Gorge, in west Africa, was first explored by a scientist in 1911 when a German called Doctor Kattwinkel (honest!) went looking for butterflies, not bones. He picked up some curious fossil bones and sent them back to Germany to be examined. The Germans were excited by the discovery and sent archaeologists out to dig. Olduvai Gorge became one of the greatest areas for finding fossil hominids.

When the archaeologists started digging it's certain they didn't use caterpillar tractors. (Caterpillar – butterfly! Geddit? Oh, never mind.)

4 Walk the dog
The German investigations were interrupted by the First World War. A British family moved in, the Leakey family (Louis, Mary and their son Richard), and made some of the greatest discoveries of all time. But they still needed a lot of Kattwinkel's luck.

The Leakeys found lots of animal bones and stone tools but no human remains, though they searched for 30 years. Then one morning Mary took her Dalmatian dogs for a walk away from the camp. She saw bones sticking out from the ground where rains had washed away the soil. They were the bones of the oldest man ever found. He was nicknamed 'Nutcracker Man' because of his powerful teeth.

IT MUST HAVE RAINED KATTWINKELS AND DOGS! BOOM! BOOM!

IF THEY WERE DALMATIANS, THEY PROBABLY 'SPOTTED' THE BONES FIRST! HO! HO!

NUTCRACKER MAN LIVES ON... IN THIS VERY ROOM

5 Raft craft

In 1912 the adventurous sons of Count Begouen decided to explore an underground river called the Volp. (Warning: don't explore underground rivers like the Volp. If you get trapped you'll not get any holp.)

The boys used gas bottles as floats and wooden crates to build a raft on top. Their boat drifted into a cave. They reached a cliff and climbed it up to a gallery. They discovered some ancient cave art in the gallery and moved on.

The passage became a chimney in the rock which they struggled up – into a second gallery that hadn't been seen by humans since the last Ice Age.

The boys spotted claw marks of cave bears, old bones and even Stone Age footprints on the damp floor. They also found clay models of bison – the first ever find of Stone Age sculptures.

The case of the exploding coffin

Accidents don't *always* help archaeologists. Sometimes accidents happen to these daring diggers ... and they can be pretty gruesome, as this story from the north-east of England shows.

Dear Erica,

Don't laugh. It isn't funny. I know you've heard the story from our friends but you should hear my side of the story.

As you know we were up here investigating a medieval cemetery when we came across a wooden coffin. It took us most of the day to raise it to the side of the trench. We lowered it to the ground but a rope slipped and it had a bumpy landing. That's when we heard a hissing sound coming from the coffin. The professor cried 'Run!' and we turned our backs and scattered for cover.

I guess I was about ten metres from the coffin when it exploded. Something soft smacked into the back of my jacket. The blast blew me forward on to my hands and knees but I wasn't hurt, you'll be pleased to hear.

I stood up and took off my jacket to see what had hit me. I stared at the jacket and the jacket stared back! A medieval eyeball had been blown from the corpse and hit me. For some reason my so-called friends thought this was hilarious! But no one offered to pull the eyeball off!

That's not the end of the story. I had to give a talk to a local church society about our excavations in their graveyard. I explained, 'The gases given off by the rotting body combined with the lead lining of the coffin to make an explosive gas!'

An old lady in the second row stood up, shaking like a leaf, and moaning, 'Ooooh! Me uncle Albert's buried in a lead-lined coffin! Is he going to explode?'

She had a picture of exploding coffins popping off in every graveyard in the country!

As I say, it is NOT funny. But you have to laugh.

See you soon.

Love

Annie

But there are worse things than exploding coffins for some archaeologists. One disaster is being proved wrong, as this sad story shows...

Dead drop

Archaeologists are making new discoveries all the time. Some of these prove that the old ideas were mistaken. This is bad luck if you've spent a lifetime teaching students one thing only to discover you were wrong all along. That's what happened to one famous archaeologist in Austria in 1957...

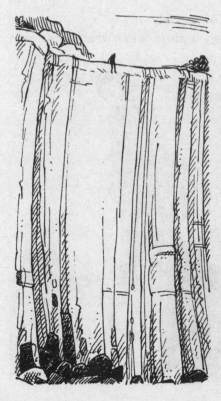

The old man lowered himself on to the ledge and looked down at the sheer drop below him. In the fading light the boulders far below him looked like pebbles. His feet hung over the edge and he shuffled forward till all that stopped him from tumbling over were his hands on the dusty trail.

He didn't see the young woman with the rucksack rounding the bend in the trail. 'Hey!' she cried. 'Be careful! You'll fall!'

The old man didn't turn or look at her. His

lank grey hair blew in the warm summer evening air and his thin body seemed to sway. The girl with the nut-brown skin knew there was something wrong. She dropped her rucksack on to the path and stepped carefully towards the man. He shifted forward till he was perched on the very edge. She stopped. She licked her dry lips and said quietly, 'No.'

For a long time they both remained still. Then the old man spoke in a firm voice. 'Good evening.'

'Good evening. Nice evening,' she replied nervously. 'I'm Ellie Griffiths.'

'And my name is Katz. Professor Gerhardt Katz. You may have heard of me?'

'No,' she said quickly. Too quickly.

He frowned. 'There was a time when that name was known around the world.'

'Really?'

'Really. For 40 years I was one of the most respected names in archaeology, you know. My books were used by colleges all over the world.'

'Wow,' Ellie said gently. 'I'll have to look out for them.'

'Don't bother,' the man said, suddenly bitter. He turned and looked at her for the first time.

She squatted on the ground and smiled. 'Tell me about them.'

He sighed. 'I looked at all the evidence and I came up with a new idea. I proved that 3,000 years ago the climate of the world became warmer and drier. There was a terrible drought across the Earth. The hunters couldn't wander across the deserts of the Middle East. All the animals would gather at a watering-hole – what they call an oasis. So human hunters began to gather at these watering holes.'

'That makes sense,' the girl nodded.

The old man stared into the empty sky and went on eagerly: 'I could see what would happen next. Stone Age humans stopped being wandering hunters and they began to settle. They built houses and the houses gathered into villages and the villages became the world's first cities. They planted crops, they herded sheep and goats.'

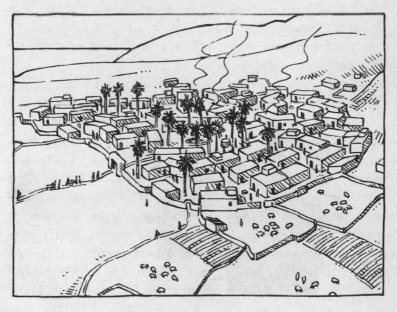

'They made the world's first farms,' Ellie nodded and shifted slightly so she was closer to the man on the edge.

'That's what I told the world. I gave lectures on every continent. No one was more famous than me in archaeology. No one!' he said and sighed.

'What went wrong?' the girl asked and rested her weight on one hand. She used it to pull herself closer.

'A man called Libby had worked on the atomic bombs that could destroy the world in 1945. Then in 1949 he created the bomb that destroyed me. He invented carbon dating. Ever heard of it?'

'Yes. It's a way of telling how old things are,' the girl murmured.

'Suddenly archaeologists had a way of telling how old their finds were. A woman called Kathleen Kenyon was digging at Jericho and found an early farm village. Of course she was able to carbon-date it. Farmers worked there in 7,500 BC! Imagine that! They'd been farming thousands of years before I'd said they had. My life's work was ruined! Ruined!'

The man moaned and shifted forward so he barely sat on the ledge. If he leaned forward he would be gone. Ellie Griffiths held her breath. Then she whispered, 'No! You were right about the other things!'

'One by one my ideas were destroyed. Farming didn't start at the watering-holes – it started in Palestine. And they didn't plant crops. Not for 2,000 years.

They simply stayed in one place and learned to live off the wild grasses that grew there every year – they didn't plough and plant seeds the way I said they had. I was wrong, wrong, wrong!' he moaned.

Ellie edged closer. She couldn't think what to say. He turned suddenly and stared at her wildly, his faded eyes filled with tears. 'My whole life has been wasted! You see why I have to do this!'

'No.'

'I used to walk here when I was a young man. I know this place well. No one who goes over the edge ever comes back. No one. Wasted. Whole life.'

Ellie reached out a hand and her fingertips brushed the sleeve of his jacket. He snatched his arm away, twisted and gave a small sob as he fell. The girl grasped at the air where the old man had been.

It was a long time before she could move, before she could bring herself to look over the ledge to the pitiless rocks below.

Super science
The old archaeologist committed suicide because new methods of archaeology were making his books look out of date. Yet many of his ideas were brilliant and are still studied today.

The carbon-14 dating system that upset him so much was indeed invented by nuclear bomb scientists. They found that...

- All living plants are bombarded by radioactivity from outer space.
- Anything that eats vegetables takes on the radioactivity. (Yes! That includes *you*!)

- You have one of these carbon-14 atoms for every trillion ordinary carbon atoms.
- After death, this radioactive material (carbon-14) takes about 5,568 years for half of it to go away.
- So if an archaeologist digs up a plant or animal that has half its carbon-14 then it is 5,568 years old. Geddit?

If you want to try counting trillions of carbon atoms to find the carbon-14 then you can.

It's easier to let a machine called an *accelerator mass spectrometer* do it. All you need is a few million dollars to buy it and a few million volts of electricity to make it work!

Radiocarbon dating may be expensive ... but it could be worth it to find out if your teacher is lying about her age!

ONE, TWO, THREE, FOUR, FIVE

Silly science

On 13 May 1983 two workmen were cutting peat in a bog when they uncovered a dead body. The police were told about it and the find was reported in the newspapers.

A local man came forward and confessed that he had murdered his wife and disposed of her body in the bog back in 1960. He went to prison for the crime. But archaeologists who examined the body said that this particular corpse was almost 2,000 years old. They used radiocarbon dating.

Oooops! The man had got away with murder for 23 years and the bog body made him panic into going to the police. His wife's corpse is still missing.

Or is it...? In 1998 a row broke out over the dead head.

29 March 1998 — £2·50

Archaeology Weekly

BIG BATTLE OVER BOG BODY

'MUSEUM EXPERTS ARE MUGS' SAYS TOP DOC

Archaeologists at the British Museum are furious over reports that they've made a major mistake. A head that they dated as being 2,000 years old is said to be the victim of a 38-year-old murder.

In 1960 Edmund Roberts murdered his wife Maria and hid the body in Lindow bog. Police suspected him but couldn't prove he'd anything to do with his wife's disappearance. Then, in 1983, two peat-diggers uncovered a body and Roberts owned up. 'It's my wife. I killed her and buried her there,' he said.

He was sentenced to life imprisonment even though British Museum scientists dated the corpse using the radiocarbon method and declared, 'It's been in the bog nearly 2,000 years!'

Bog Body

Now a doctor has come forward to state that they've made a major mistake. Professor Bob Conway of Manchester University says,

'I've compared pictures of the skull with pictures of the dead woman and they match. Anyway, the body in the bog was in too good a condition to belong to an ancient Briton. There was skin attached and almost a complete eyeball. You just don't get that with an old corpse – not even one preserved in a bog.'

Lindow Bog is close to Manchester Airport and is sprayed with aircraft fuel every day. Professor Conway says that could cause the radiocarbon tests to be wildly wrong. He demanded that the British Museum should hand the skull over for further tests.

A spokesperson for the British Museum says, 'There is no chance that our tests could be wrong. The skull is in the basement of the museum and there it will stay.'

The professor and eye

Radiocarbon dating has become widely used since it was invented in 1946. Much of what historians tell us about prehistory depends on radiocarbon dating being right.

What if the method can make horrible historical mistakes? It would be disastrous for archaeology.

Why won't the museum hand over the mysterious skull? Are they afraid they may be proved *wrong*?

LOUSY LIFE

You too could live like a Stone Age person – but you'd have to give up chocolate and television. Here are a few helpful hints…

Preserving pensioners 1

The first large town in the world was probably Jericho in Palestine. The people of Stone Age Jericho (around 7,300 to 6,300 BC) seemed to love their wrinklies. They didn't stick them in an old people's home or bury them in some forgotten graveyard. No, they kept them at home, even after they were dead.

And, if they had no photographs to remind them of their glamorous granny's fabulous face, they had another way of dealing with their dead.

If there had been children's television 9,000 years ago it may have looked something like this…

1. Remember, boys and girls, always have a grown-up around if a sharp knife is being used. It's much more fun to let them cut themselves.

FIRST CAREFULLY CUT OFF THE HEAD OF THE CORPSE AND PUT IT TO ONE SIDE. THEN DIG A HOLE ABOUT ONE METRE DEEP IN THE FLOOR OF YOUR HOUSE AND BURY THE BODY

NOW REMOVE THE SKIN AND BRAINS FROM THE HEAD TILL YOU ARE LEFT WITH A CLEAN SKULL. DON'T FORGET TO BURY THOSE BRAINS SO MUM DOESN'T HAVE TO TIDY THEM UP AFTER YOU!

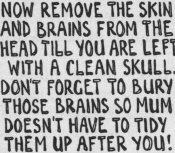

FILL THE SKULL WITH SOME OF THE PLASTER. USE MORE PLASTER TO BUILD UP THE FACE OF THE DEAD PERSON TILL IT LOOKS JUST LIKE THEY DID IN LIFE

USE TWO SHELLS FOR THE EYES AND PLACE THE HEAD ON A PLASTER STAND. HERE'S ONE I MADE EARLIER

And if the dead person had a moustache when he (or she) was alive, then you could paint a moustache on to the clay head.

Some archaeologists believe the whole body was buried for a few months until the flesh was rotten. Then it was dug up again and the head removed. The rotten flesh would fall off the skull and make it easier to clean. This is a nice job for someone with no sense of smell.

One group of four Palestine heads were buried together. It looks as if a couple of children were taken to the funeral and sacrificed to the dead. That's one way of keeping class sizes down, I suppose.

Preserving pensioners 2

Around 3,000 BC the Egyptians started turning their dead kings and queens into mummies. But they weren't the first people to make mummies. Three thousand years before – and on the other side of the world – one group of Stone Age people were making very different types of mummies.

Between 6,000 and 1,500 BC the Chinchorro people of northern Chile were mummifying their dead. The special skills must have been passed down from parents to children. It would have been easier if they'd had schools, exercise books and teachers, of course...

73

Making a mummy just like
Mummy used to make

1. First cut off the head, arms and legs. (Handy hint: make sure the person is dead first.)

2. Skin the body parts and put the skin ~~too~~ to one side to be used later on. (Handy hint: skin on legs can be rolled down like stockings.)

3. Empty the body of all the soft parts and fill it with hot coals or sand to dry it out. (Handy hint: don't make the coals too hot or you'll have cooked corpse.)

4. Slice open the arms and legs, take out the bones, scrape and clean them. (Handy hint: make sure your pet dog doesn't chew on the bones.)

5. Lash sticks to the bones and replace them. Place long sticks inside the body to attach the legs, arms and head. (Handy hint: a good mummy will be so stiff it can stand as straight as you.)

6. Pack the body with grass and ashes so

it looks the same shape as it was when it was alive. (Handy hint: use cold ashes or you'll set fire to the grass and end up with a charred Chinchorro.)

7. Assemble the body and cover it with a paste made from white ash. Model it to the shape of the dead person — including the face and the naughty bits. (Handy hint: wash your hands after handling the naughty bits.)

8. Put the skin back over the body. Don't forget the hair on the head. (Handy ~~bit~~ hint: check for nits.)

9. Paint the whole body in black using special paint. Use different colours for the eyes, lips and eyebrows. (Handy hint: use your mother's make-up...or your father's.)

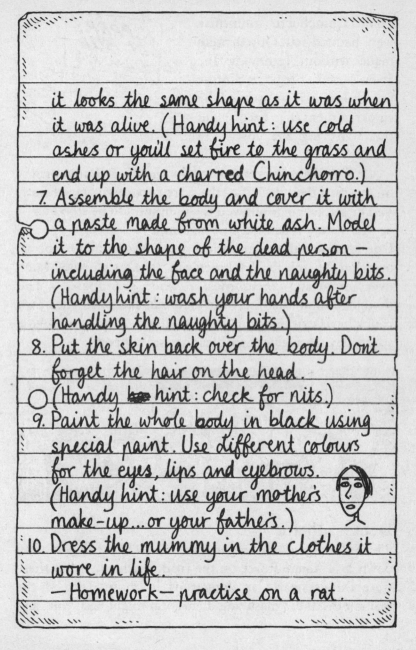

10. Dress the mummy in the clothes it wore in life.

— Homework — practise on a rat.

Some Chinchorro mummies were painted red. Others were made without removing the arms and legs. Simple mummies were preserved by smoking them (like bacon) and then covering the corpse in mud.

We'll probably never know why the Chinchorro people mummified their dead, but there are two interesting clues...
- The sticks inside allowed the mummies to be stood up.
- Many were repainted several times.

One idea is that the mummies were taken out for special occasions so the dead Chinchorro ancestors could watch over important ceremonies. If your grandparents had thought of mummifying your Victorian ancestors, then they could be taken along to your wedding ... or your school sports day ... to give their blessing and support!

Doctor, doctor!

The Stone Age was a dangerous age. No chance of being run down by a Range Rover on the road to school ... but there were things nearly as dangerous in those days. If the mammoths didn't mash you then a bear might bash you, and all you'd have to defend yourself with would be flint-headed arrows and spears.

Animal attacks, accidents and illnesses could kill you before you could say, 'Is there a doctor in the cave?' What were the chances of finding a doctor in the Stone Age? Surprisingly good ... and they probably didn't have six-month waiting lists!

Could you be a Neanderthal nurse or a Stone Age surgeon? Try matching the sickness to the cure...

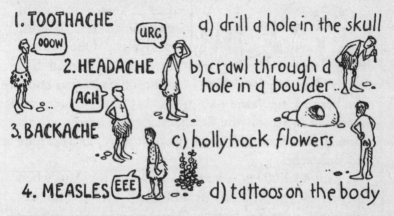

1. TOOTHACHE *OOOW* *URG*   a) drill a hole in the skull

2. HEADACHE   b) crawl through a hole in a boulder

AGH

3. BACKACHE   c) hollyhock flowers

4. MEASLES *EEE*   d) tattoos on the body

Answers:

1c) All the types of flowers found in a Neanderthal grave in Iraq have been used to make medicines in modern times. So they probably weren't just put there for decoration – they were put there to help the corpse in the next life. Hollyhocks were used to cure toothache. Obviously there are no dentists in the afterlife so we have that to look forward to!

2a) The first brain surgeons lived in the New Stone Age. They were able to peel back the scalp with stone knives

then drill holes in the skull with a sharp flint drill. This would be used to release the pressure of a swollen brain or to fix a caved-in skull. Most of the victims would die after this sort of operation, but a few survived. One skull showed that a man had survived *seven* holes drilled in his head! (Scientists know this because the bone had grown back.) The hole was supposed to let out the devils inside the head and this surgery is still used by some people for things as simple as a headache.

3d) Around 3,000 BC a man was crossing the Alps when he was caught in a storm and died. His corpse was preserved in ice and discovered by hikers in 1991. It's the oldest fully preserved human body ever found. It would have been in perfect condition if the workmen sent to collect him hadn't used a pneumatic drill to break him from the ice and shattered his hip. They also managed to break his arm by forcing him into a coffin. X-rays show he had arthritis that would have made his neck and back ache. There are tattoos on his leathery skin – parallel, vertical blue lines on both sides of his spine where he must have felt pain. It seems likely that the tattoos were meant to cure the back pain. There is no cure for pains in the neck who attack you with pneumatic drills!

4b) Some stones have natural holes in them and children are still sent to crawl through the holes as a cure for things like measles, whooping cough and other diseases. We can guess that this custom goes back to the Stone Age when the stones were set up inside a stone circle. At Dingwall in the Scottish Highlands the child's clothes are passed through the hole first and then the child. Imagine how embarrassed you'd be!

Terrible trepanning

Drilling a hole in the skull to cure a brain problem is called 'trepanning'. It seems crazy and cruel to us. You may think it's the sort of thing only a Stone-Ager could do. You'd be wrong!

In 1962, the Dutch doctor Bart Hughes put forward the idea that a hole in the skull keeps you young. He used an electric drill to make a hole in his own head. He survived the drilling but was locked away in a Dutch mental hospital.

But three years later a British student, Joe Mallam, met the daft Dutch doctor and decided to try trepanning for himself. He had a painkilling injection in the scalp (which Stone-Agers didn't have) but he had no help – the Dutch doc was refused entry into Britain ... probably because Britain already has enough mad doctors.

At his first attempt, Joe collapsed and ended up in hospital. But the next time he succeeded. You don't want to know what happened next. Skip the rest of this section and go on to the next ... or have a sick-bucket handy. Joe described his scientific breakthrough – or his skull-entific breakthrough.

> *After some time there was a grim sounding schlurp and the sound of bubbling. I drew the drill out and the gurgling continued. It sounded like, air bubbles rising under the skull as they were pressed out. I looked at the drill and there was a bit of bone in it. At last! If only I had an electric drill it would have been much simpler. I bandaged up my head and cleared away the mess.*

Don't try this at home ... even if your dad's bald spot *does* look in need of a hole.

Fighting farmers

By 5,000 BC Stone-Agers had begun to settle in Europe to farm the land. The wandering hunters stopped wandering, stayed in one place and built villages, herded cattle, planted crops and made pottery.

Peaceful. Right?

Wrong.

Many of the villages were protected by ditches and wooden walls. Historians guessed that the farmers had to protect themselves against the Stone-Agers who hadn't settled – the ones who still wandered the land, hunting animals and gathering plants.

But the historians were just *guessing*. The truth was finally discovered in 1983. A man in Talheim, Germany, was digging in his garden when he uncovered some bones ... human bones!

The man told the police, who realized the bones were ancient. They called in the archaeologists, who made some gruesome discoveries.

- there were 34 skeletons in a pit
- they had all died violently
- most of them had their skulls smashed by clubs – some had a hole smashed through
- there were signs of some being hit by flint arrows
- almost half of the victims were children and one was over 60 – very old for a Stone-Ager
- seven of the adults were female

This *wasn't* a funeral site – these farming people had been massacred, then dumped there in a mass grave.

The skulls had been smashed with stone axes that the farmers used. So this *wasn't* an attack by a wandering band of hunters.

This was one farming group wiped out by another.

81

We'll never know what they argued about. Land? Animals? Mates?

But it does look as if Stone Age farmers didn't always have the peaceful life prehistorians had once imagined.

The Talheim pit shows that 7,000 years ago humans weren't just learning the special human arts of farming and making pottery. They were learning that other quaint human custom that we know so well in the 20th century – the nasty little habit of mass murder.

When you're fighting a war being right doesn't matter. It is winning![1]

Dead unlucky

In prehistoric USA there was a massacre of a tribe in what is now known as South Dakota. There were few women and children found by archaeologists amongst the skeletons, so they may have been taken prisoner.

Many of the bodies had been chopped up after death – the hands and feet cut off and the heads scalped so the winners could take the hair as a prize.

But the unluckiest man was one who had been scalped a few years before the attack. His head had healed and he'd survived that first scalping. He must have thought his luck was in until the sad slap-head was attacked and scalped again.

He didn't survive the second time.

1. Actual words spoken by a mass murderer 7,000 years after the Talheim massacre. Imagine that! The mind of a Stone-Ager in the body of a 20th century national leader. There aren't any of those around today ... are there?

ROTTEN RITUALS

If you lived in the Stone Age, then you worried about the weather. A bad harvest meant starvation. There were no Stone Age supermarkets to stock up your larder.

The weather is a matter of luck. But the Stone-Agers believed there were ways you could bring yourself good luck in this life and the next life.

The ancient Greeks and Egyptians had their 'gods'. But Stone-Agers seemed to worship their dead ancestors whose spirits had travelled to an afterlife.

It was important to keep your dead ancestors happy. Look after their spirits and the spirits will look after you.

First you had to release the spirit from the dead body it is trapped in. The spirit could only leave when the flesh is falling off the bones. So, you can wait till your friend's/Dad's/teacher's corpse has gone mouldy and then bury it. If you want to speed things up you can help him or her by hacking the flesh off the body with a stone knife or leaving it outside for animals and birds to pick clean.

In Denmark, there are marks on one corpse that show it was scalped before death. This could have been to let the spirit out – or it could have been an attempt by a hungry

Stone-Ager to get *in* and steal the brain to eat it. (Minced up with a small onion and fried, you'd have a tasty Stone-Age brain-burger! Yummy!)

Of course, keeping the spirits happy needed some revolting rituals...

Funeral stew

On Anglesey, in Wales, there's a stone burial chamber called Barclodiad y Gawres. Archaeologists have worked out the revolting ritual that went on at the funeral of two boys...

- The bodies were cremated till the flesh burned off.

- The bones were scraped, mixed with sheep bones and buried under a layer of earth.

- Inside the chamber, a fire was lit under a water pot.

- A stew was stirred into the water…

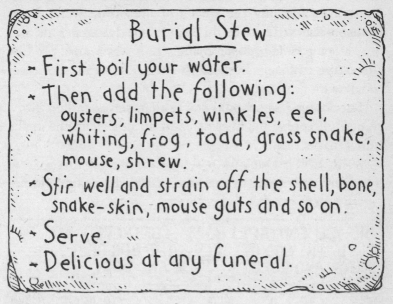

Burial Stew

- First boil your water.
- Then add the following:
  oysters, limpets, winkles, eel,
  whiting, frog, toad, grass snake,
  mouse, shrew.
- Stir well and strain off the shell, bone,
  snake-skin, mouse guts and so on.
- Serve.
- Delicious at any funeral.

The rubbish left from the tasty soup was poured on to the dying fire and trampled down to put it out.

Did you know…?
A curious custom among Australian Stone-Agers was for men to have their front two teeth knocked out. This was done when they grew up and seems to have been a sign of becoming a man.

Good manas

As well as releasing the spirits of the dead, Stone-Agers probably believed they could talk to their dead relations. But only a few people had the 'mana'. This was a word used by Stone Age professors in the 20th century. It means the power to talk with the dead.

The Stone-Agers would starve themselves and go into a trance. Of course the best place to do this would be at the burial places.

WARNING: Don't skip school dinner, go to the local graveyard and expect to chat to Elvis Presley. It took Stone-Agers a lot of practice to get 'mana'.

Christians who worship in a church today have their dead buried all around them in the churchyard. But Stone-Agers often buried the bones of their dead in one place and worshipped in another. In western Europe you would walk up a long straight path edged with stones until you reached your temple – a stone circle like the mighty Stonehenge...

Horrible henges

Archaeologists can explain how Stonehenge was built in the days before cranes and bulldozers. They've experimented with raising stones using ropes and wood. They can tell you when it was built and show how it used to look. But they *can't* agree on what happened inside the stone circle. There have been some strange ideas:

But no Egyptian remains have ever been found there. So let's forget *that* idea.

But Stonehenge is much older than 1,600 BC. Forget *that* idea too.

Would you Adam-and-Eve it? (That's Cockney rhyming slang for 'believe it', okey dokey?) That charming idea was put forward in 1943 by a Scotsman who maybe had porridge instead of brains.

Errr ... *you* may like to believe that. People with half a brain read on and see some more likely ideas.

True history of the henge

It became a deserted holy place. Huge stone graves (long barrows) were scattered over the plain and were filled with skeletons. But the heads were removed and buried in a sacred enclosure on Windmill Hill where rituals took place.

After hundreds of years the heads in the ditches were abandoned and the Stone-Agers went back to the old site of the three poles, where they built a circular ditch – a 'henge' – with earth banks.

A RING OF WOODEN POSTS WAS PUT ROUND THE OUTSIDE. THIS WAS A PLACE WHERE THE DEAD AND THE LIVING COULD MEET

SO THIS IS THE DEAD CENTRE OF SALISBURY PLAIN!

The moon was special to these henge people. Maybe they thought it was a place where the spirits of the dead went, or where spirits came from. The stone circle seems to have been used to measure the movement of the moon in the sky. Posts marked the spot where the moon rose at its most southerly point.

THE TIMBER CIRCLE WAS REMOVED AFTER 50 YEARS AND A ROUND WOODEN TEMPLE WAS BUILT. CREMATED HUMAN REMAINS WERE FOUND IN THE OUTSIDE DITCH IN LINE WITH THE RISING MOON. THEY HELD SERVICES FOR THE DEAD HERE. LIKE A CHURCH

DAD TOOK OUR CAR FOR A SERVICE

HOW DID HE GET IT UP THE CHURCH STEPS?

Every month the full moon disappears to nothing then grows again. It dies and comes back to life. Maybe the Stone-Agers thought humans were like that! They die then they are born again … then die and are born again … and so on!

And maybe, they thought, the living humans can use the power of the moon to help the dead of the tribe to be reborn. Of course when *you* die then the tribe will do the same for *you*. That seems like a fair deal, doesn't it? Worship your ancestors, worship the moon and your spirit will never die.

AROUND 2500BC THE WOODEN TEMPLE WAS REPLACED BY THE STONE CIRCLE—THE ONE THAT IS STILL LARGELY THERE TODAY. TWO MORE CIRCLES OF HOLES WERE DUG OUTSIDE STONEHENGE READY TO TAKE NEW STONES. THEY WERE NEVER FILLED. STONEHENGE WAS NEVER EVER FINISHED!

JUST LIKE YOUR HOMEWORK, DARREN GRINT!

Later the sun became as important as the moon and its positions at the solstices were marked by a stone called a 'heel' stone. A straight avenue leads up to Stonehenge and if you walk up it on the shortest day of the year you can see the sun set exactly ahead of you.

Picture the scene in Stone Age times. The days have been getting shorter for six months – if they keep on getting shorter then the sun will vanish for good and everyone will die! But after that important day (21 December) the dying days grow longer again. Phew!

There you have it again. Death followed by birth.

21 December is the edge of time. This was the time of the year when the walls between life and death were weak. This

was the time that the people with the 'mana' could talk to the ancestors.

TODAY SOME PEOPLE BELIEVE THIS SORT OF THING HAPPENS ON 31 OCTOBER, THE DAY WE CALL HALLOWE'EN, WHEN SPIRITS AND WITCHES WANDER THE NIGHT

SHE SHOULD KNOW

The people who came after the Stone-Agers stopped believing in ancestor spirits. They believed in spirits in water and sacred groves of trees instead. Around 1,500 BC Stonehenge was abandoned after being used for 1,500 years – longer than any of today's churches and cathedrals.

SO, THERE YOU HAVE IT! STONEHENGE IS A GIANT CALENDAR AND, ONCE A YEAR, A DOORWAY TO THE WORLD OF GHOSTS

I STILL THINK IT'S A LAUNCH PAD FOR UFOS

Henge head-scratchers
A modern archaeologist has said…

Most of what has been written about Stonehenge is nonsense!

Here is some of that nonsense in a simple quiz for simple stone brains. Stonehenge has seen a lot of curious things in 5,000 years – and they're not all nonsense. But can you tell which facts are false and which are true?

1 Stonehenge was close to being destroyed in an air crash.

2 The 'Altar Stone' was given its name by the Stone-Agers who used it for sacrifices.

3 Stonehenge was built in a circle to make the music played inside sound better.

4 Stonehenge was built by the high priests of the Celtic people – the Druids.

5 Some of the Stonehenge stones are set in concrete.

6 In 1920 an archaeologist excavated under the Slaughter Stone. He found a bottle of port wine.

7 The Romans came to Stonehenge and knocked some of the stones down.

8 Stonehenge is a giant computer that can be used to calculate when there will be an eclipse of the sun.

Answers:
1 True. Accidents have helped to uncover some of the greatest archaeology finds. But they have also come close to destroying them! In 1910 Horatio Barber designed a new aeroplane. He chose his chauffeur as the test pilot.

The chauffeur had never flown an aeroplane before, but the brilliant Barber said...

You can drive my cars, you can drive my aeroplane.

Flying a plane is just a bit more difficult than driving a car ... as the poor chauffeur found out. The ASL Monoplane took off from Larkhill near Stonehenge ... narrowly missed demolishing it, and was wrecked close by.

There was a story that the army wanted Stonehenge torn down because it was a danger to their airmen.

When the First World War started four years later in 1914, part of Stonehenge *was* destroyed, but not by enemy action or by low-flying loonies. The British Army set up a huge camp on Salisbury Plain that spread over the ditch around the stone circle and ruined any chance of archaeologists finding anything there.

YOU WOULDN'T BELIEVE IT SARGE. I SITS DOWN TO 'AVE ME TEA, AN' I GETS AN ARROW'EAD IN ME BUM!

2 False. 'Altar Stone' was a name invented by people who liked to imagine there'd been bloodthirsty rituals at Stonehenge. But the 'Altar Stone' was set upright in the

ground when the Stone-Agers built Stonehenge. Anyone wanting to make a sacrifice on the 'Altar Stone' would have had to get the victim up a long pair of ladders!

Stonehenge also has a 'Slaughter Stone' where people weren't slaughtered, a 'Heel Stone' with a mark like a heel-print that isn't a heel-print. It even has two 'Station Stones' ... and no train has ever stopped there!

3 True ... if you believe scientists at Southampton University. They say sounds would bounce off the stones and they could act like giant amplifiers. Drums played in a Stone Age ceremony would boom around and sound as exciting as a modern pop concert.

4 False. Everyone confuses the Druids with Stonehenge. That's because Druids, with their long white beards and longer white robes, have used the stone circle for over 2,000 years and they still use it today. But Stonehenge was there 2,000 years before them!

The 'Ancient order of Druids' isn't all that ancient. It

was founded in 1781 as a sort of secret society for over-grown boys. Apart from the magical meetings and secret ceremonies they helped each other out with much more simple, day-to-day problems. Their secret newspaper made special offers like…

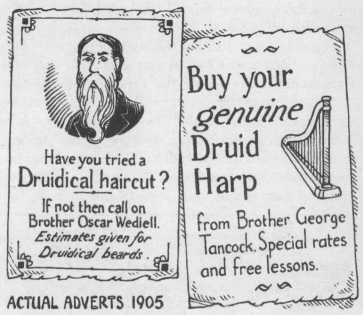

Have you tried a
Druidical haircut?
If not then call on
Brother Oscar Wediell.
Estimates given for
Druidical beards.

Buy your
genuine
Druid
Harp

from Brother George
Tancock. Special rates
and free lessons.

ACTUAL ADVERTS 1905

The modern Druids held their first great feast at Stonehenge in 1905 when about 700 turned up. A rival group of Druids also turned up in 1905 but were in trouble when they refused to pay the entrance fee to get in and tried to bury the ashes of dead members in the middle of the circle.

The Druids were banned in 1926 and cursed the caretaker who kept them out. The man died soon after and the Druids said, 'See what you get!' But they gave up; some Druids planned to build a full-size copy of

Stonehenge about a mile away, some went to worship at the Tower of London, but most simply agreed to pay to get in.

5 True. But it isn't Stone Age concrete – the Stone-Agers hadn't invented it. They placed the stones in pits, packed them with rubble and connected them to each other with clever joints.

The stones began to fall down in recent times and when modern archaeologists replaced them they set them in concrete. During the First World War the British army tested bombs on Salisbury Plain that made the stones shake and wobble. Tanks rumbled past just five metres from the circle. No wonder they needed patching up when the war ended. The Stone-Agers who put the stones up never dreamed of bombs, aeroplanes, tanks and tourists coming to wreck their hard work.

In 1963 one of the stones was so wobbly it blew down in a gale. But a lot of modern houses blew down in the same gale and they hadn't been around for 5,000 years! The Stone-Agers would have been proud of that.

6 True. It wasn't Stone Age port wine. The bottle had

been left there in 1810 by the last person to dig beneath the stone. Sadly the cork had rotted and most of the wine had seeped out.

But there were deadlier things left beneath the stones than a bottle of port wine. In 1723 the owner was Thomas Hayward and he brought rabbits to Stonehenge. They would make nice pies, he thought. Unfortunately, the rotten rabbits didn't want to be made into pies so they dug themselves long burrows into the soil beneath the stones. The burrows collapsed and the stones began to fall. Some of the falling stones may have crushed the wrecking rabbits and their burrows – but maybe they should have hit the hopeless Hayward!

7 False. The Romans are often blamed for ruining Stonehenge. Even in the 1950s *The Times* newspaper was pointing a finger of blame at Roman wreckers. It's just not true. The Romans *did* come to Stonehenge – but stones like the one known as number 55 had already fallen *before* they arrived. 'How on earth do the archaeologists know *that*?' you ask in amazement. (Go on. Ask, and I'll tell you.)

The Romans probably camped there while they built their road over Salisbury Plain. They dropped coins and tools and bits of uniform and pottery, the way Romans do. Archaeologists found Roman bits and bobs all *around* fallen stone 55 but none *underneath* it. Why? Because the stone was already flattened before they got there.

Archaeologists are sometimes like detectives. If Sherlock Holmes finds a corpse lying on dry ground on a rainy day then he says, 'Aha! This corpse was deaded *before* it started to rain! Elementary, my dear Watson!' And that's how sensible archaeologists know about the flattening of 55. Dumb archaeologists have argued the Romans ruined Stonehenge – some have even said Stonehenge was *built* by the Romans. But you know better. (In any case, carbon-dating has proved it's Stone Age.)

> *My discovery of the Roman origins of Stonehenge is one of the triumphs of modern ~~arki~~ ~~archeagogy~~ ~~archy~~ ~~archeolotic~~ ~~stuff~~ digging up of old stuff!*

8 Errrr … probably false. A very clever professor wrote a book in which he tried to prove that Stone-Agers placed the stones so the shadows acted like a calendar. But the very clever professor had books and calculators to help him. The Stonehenge Stone-Agers didn't even have writing. All that knowledge would have to be kept in their heads and passed down by word of mouth. The builders were clever, but not that clever.

The day of the Druid
For ten years British police banned all visitors from Stonehenge on the longest and shortest days of the year. This followed the 'Battle of the Bean Field' in 1985 when police battled with travellers arriving for a mid-summer festival.

Then in December 1997 and June 1998 just a hundred people were allowed back to worship the sun on those days. They were guarded by a ring of 500 policemen who tried to keep out troublemakers. The police had missed a small group who had crawled four miles in darkness to sneak into the circle before the sunrise. Troublemakers in Salisbury, led by a man who called himself 'King Arthur', had been arrested the night before.

The worshippers followed the beliefs of the Celtic Druids, and there were black witches there too. At 4:52 a.m. the worshippers turned to the Heel Stone to see the sunlight flood over the ancient site. 'Hail ye, O Sun!' the chief Druid called.

But it was a cloudy morning and the sun didn't appear. Everyone wished one another 'Happy solstice' anyway.

A young couple held a pagan wedding. Their wrists were joined with a loop of red wool while they jumped over a crystal and a bunch of flowers. They kissed and that meant they were married for a year and a day.

After a few hours of chanting, dancing and hugging stones the group started to leave. *Then* the sun came out! 'Hail ye, O Sun!' everyone cried and went home.

Harmless amusement. But what would the ancient Stone Age worshippers at Stonehenge have made of it all? They had abandoned the site hundreds of years before Celtic Druids were even thought of.

They might have smiled at the curious Druids, but they would have been amazed to see the chief Druid climb into his chariot and drive off. Because his chariot was a battered and rusty Austin Montego car!

White cow, black witch

Stonehenge is one of the most famous stone circles in the world. But it isn't the only one and it certainly isn't the largest one.

Many of the other stone circles have stories to explain their existence. They are believed to be lucky places where the goodness of nature is concentrated.

(Note to readers: The following story is to be read aloud in one of those strong country yokel accents with plenty of your own 'Ooooh-arrrrhhhhs!' sprinkled around. Try and find some snotty little infant to tell it to. They may sneer, but just remember – seriously grown-up adults invented this story in the dim and distant past to explain a stone circle on the Welsh–English border!)

Never go to Mitchell's Fold in Shropshire, me dears, not if you values your life! Ye will see an old stone circle there, me dears. Beware! Don't you not be going near it! For there be a witch there, me dears, and she be trapped inside the biggest stone in the circle!

Ye see, it all starts with a strange white cow – you know the sort? It's just like a black cow only white. Anyway, there's this terrible famine throughout the land and everybody they be starving and dying of hunger, they be. When along comes this white cow and plonks herself in the middle of the old stone circle. This there white cow lets everyone take a bucket of milk and she never runs dry. Them there buckets of milk saves the lives of the villagers.

MUNCH MUNCH

But the cow warns them (she's a talking cow, see?), she warns them, 'If any of you greedy beggars takes more than a bucketful, I'll go away and never come back!' She's a huffy cow you see, me dears?

Then one dark night a spiteful witch comes along. The white cow can't see what's going on 'cos it's dark, it being night an' all. And the witch is milking the white cow into a sieve! Well! The milk runs out, doesn't it?

Suddenly there's a flash of lightning (did I mention there were a thunderstorm brewing? No? Well there were). Anyway, the cow sees the sieve in the light of the flash and gets fair mad as a bull with a red rag ('cos cows is a bit like bulls).

The mad cow kicks the witch who turns into a stone and there she stands to this very day. Then the cow vanishes and never comes back – and there she *doesn't* stand to this very day.

The thunderstorm brought an end to the drought that caused the famine and the people had food and didn't need no never-ending milk no more and they all lives happy ever after, don't they? (Ooooh-aaaarrrrhhhh!)

But they still remember that there white cow in Mitchell's Fold.

Which just goes to show.

Something.

Many stone circle legends say the stones were once people or animals. Others say stones were…

A complete wedding party, turned to stone for dancing on a Sunday (Stanton Drew, Avon, England)

Three women who sinned by working on a Sunday (Moelfre Hill, Wales)

A robber caught stealing from a church (various places)

Giants who refused to be christened when Christianity came to the land (Western Isles of Scotland)

Women who gave false evidence that led to a man being hanged (Cottrell, South Wales)

A girl running away from a wizard who wanted to marry her (Aberdeen, Scotland)

A cow, a witch and a fisherman (Inisbofin, Ireland)

A giant and his seven sons who went to war with a wizard (Kerry, Ireland)

A mermaid's children (Cruckancornia, Ireland)

A history teacher who gave impossibly hard homework and was turned to stone by a pupil with witch powers ... you wish!

Cwaint henge customs

Many henges and Stone Age sites still have odd beliefs attached to them. Here are a few you may like to try ... if you are a seriously sad person.

1 Want to know if a sick friend will live? Go to Brahan Woods near Dingwall in Scotland and find the stone circle. Bring some cakes to the circle and leave them overnight. If the cakes are gone the next morning your friend will survive. But if the cakes are still there ... call the undertaker (or the under-caker!).

2 Want to win the lottery? Go to any Irish stone circle and take a cow with you. Cut the cow and let some blood out into a cup. Drink some of the blood and pour the rest into the soil. This will bring you luck – unless the cow is upset by the bleeding and sends you flying when you bend over to pour its blood away! This bloody custom was still being carried out in Queen Victoria's day.

3 Want to know who you'll marry? If you are a girl you can go to Arthur's Stone at Gower near Swansea, Wales. Wait till midnight when the moon is full and put cakes, milk and honey on the ancient stone. Crawl round the stone three times on your hands and knees. If the vision of your lover appears then you will marry him. If not, then he's probably too busy watching the telly. Of course this only works for

girls. Boys can simply follow the girls with a video camera and catch them crawling round in circles (which is much more fun and less painful).

4 Want your own private jet/yacht/bicycle? Go to Ben Loyal in Scotland and find the 'Stone of the Little Men'. Place a silver coin with a model or a drawing of any metal object you want. In a week's time you'll find a perfect one made by the little men who live under the stone.

5 Can you count the stones in a circle? Many stone circles are said to be so magical you can't actually count the number of stones there. (Mind you, some people have trouble counting the fingers on one hand!) Several stone circles have legends about bakers laying a loaf of bread on each stone to help them count them. A loaf always seemed to go missing and spoil the plan. In one story a baker stood up and said, 'The number of stones in the circle is ... cccct!' and he dropped down dead before he could announce it.

Hanging around the henge

Stonehenge was the only Stone Age circle known by early historians. Other circles were buried or destroyed or not seen.

'Not seen?' I hear you gasp. 'How can a dirty great ring of blooming big stone slabs not be *seen*?' you cry.

Well stop crying and I'll tell you.

Historians in the Middle Ages looked at them and said...

These circles are natural objects. God stood them on end and put them in some sort of order. We know not why he did this.

If God stood these stones on end then he (or she) must have been pretty strong. And it must have been done on a quiet day when he wasn't creating suns, moons and stars or sending plagues of locusts to sad Stone-Agers.

Some of the stone circles like Avebury in Wiltshire, England, were so large a village was built inside the circle and the stones used to make the houses.[1] That sort of destruction made many circles hard to spot. But there was never any confusion about Stonehenge – only arguments about *who* had built it and *why* it had been built.

'Stonehenge' was given its name in the Old English language. The 'Stone' half of the name meant 'stone'. (I'll bet you'd never have guessed that!) But what did some people say the 'henge' part of the word meant?

It was Old English for...

a) circle

b) stool

c) gallows

1. Avebury is 425 metres across – the ditch round 'little' Stonehenge is just 100 metres across.

The counting king

Stonehenge was visited by King James I in 1620 when he was touring the country to meet his people. James I's best friend tried to buy Stonehenge from its owner.

This was the start of the Stonehenge tourist industry. During the rest of the 17th century stones were stolen – one was used to make a bridge – or chipped to bits by visitors who wanted a souvenir lump of rock to take home. (Which is where the idea of Blackpool Rock came from. Only joking.)

In the middle of the 1600s it would cost you six pence to hire horses and a further four pence for a woman to guide you from the nearest town.

But the most famous visitor was in fear of his life when he took a day-trip to Stonehenge. He was James I's grandson, Charles – the man who would later become King Charles II. In September 1651 he was on the run from the Roundheads with a few faithful guards. If a guard had told his story then it might have gone something like this…

3 September 1650

Battle at Worcester against the Roundheads. Good name, Worcester — 'cos we came off worst-er! Me and Prince Charles had to flee before they done us like they done his dad, King Charles the first. Head on the block — chop — splatt.

Not that I'm scared of no Roundheads. It's just I'm very attached to me head. We are heading south to another country that must remain a deadly secret. We should get to France next week, Prince Charles reckons.

5 September 1651

Flitting from safe house to safe house. I'm worn out. And me boots are worn out and me bum is saddle sore. So we are resting here at Heale House in some God-forsaken place called Woodford. We're stuck in a secret room and it's doing my head in. You see we can't trust the servants. 'They'll rat on us for a sovereign!' Prince Charles reckons.

'So let's go for a ride tomorrow,' the lord of the house says. 'The servants are all at Salisbury Fair!'

A ride! What about my sore bum! Oh, well. A loyal servant (like what I am) never complains.

6 September 1651

What a strange sort of day. When all the

servants had gone me and the prince and Sir Robert Philips saddled up and rode over the hills. I never complained once about me sore bits. But I forgot about them, to be honest, when we got to this place called Stonehenge. A great circle of huge stones. Prince Charles jumps off his horse and says, 'This was the meeting place of my ancestors! The great King Brutus of the Britons! He came from Troy, you know.'

'So what was this place?' I ask.

'His palace,' Prince Charles says.

A bit draughty, I thought, what with no roof or nothing. Not the sort of palace I'd want to live in. But then Sir Robert Philips (a man with a very high opinion of himself and very smarmy to my Prince Charles if you ask me) says, 'It is said, sire, that no one can count the stones! Whenever they try they come up with a different answer every time. It is the magic of King Brutus.'

Now Prince Charles likes a bit of a challenge so he says, 'I'll bet a silver penny I can do it.' Then he turns to me and says, 'Help me, George.'

After an age Prince Charles turns to me and says, 'Well? I make it 93, George. How many did you count to?'

'Ten,' I tells him.

'Ten! There's more than ten! Why did you stop at ten?'

'Ran out of fingers,' I tells him.

Anyway he counts them again. He cries out, 'Ninety-three!' Again!'

Sir Robert Philips (did I mention he's a smarmy creep?) drops to one knee and says, 'That proves Your Majesty is the rightful heir to the throne. Only a man of Brutus's blood could count the magic stones.'

Prince Charles is pleased with that. 'The rightful king,' he says, nodding like a horse at a nose-bag. 'I'll be back!'

We rode back and hid at Heale before the servants got home. It's been a funny sort of day. But them stones is creepy – nearly as creepy as Sir Robert Philips. Definitely something magic about them. If they told my Charlie he's the rightful king then I just might believe it. He'll be back, will young Charlie. He'll be back.

And, of course, Charles returned as king within ten years. His friends were right about that – but they were wrong when they believed the circle was built by Ancient Briton King Brutus.

Stone sorcery

Many people have visited stone circles and said they 'feel' the strange power of the stones. It's not only Druids who worshipped at stone circles. Witches were said to use them as meeting places.

Of course the Christian church was worried. In AD 452 the church ordered…

You shall not worship stones!

If they were passing rules *against* it then someone must have been *doing* it!

In the village of Avebury in 1326 the Church leaders didn't just warn the villagers. They decided to do something about it – they decided to attack the stones. The question is, did the stones fight back?

'Where have all the stones gone?' the traveller asked. He wiped the drizzling rain from his eyes and peered across the muddy ditch.

A grey-haired freeman stuck his narrow, iron spade into a pile of soil, took off his wide-brimmed hat and shook the water off. He looked at the stranger through narrow eyes. 'Who're you then?'

'I'm Henry Barber the travelling surgeon. I've got leeches to suck out your bad blood and I've razors to trim your hair and beard. You must know me! I come this way every year at this time. But there's always been a great ring of stones here. Half of them have gone!' he looked around and lowered his voice. 'They say the Devil put them there. Has he taken them back again?'

The freeman rested on his spade, glad of an excuse to stop the back-breaking work but looking nervously at the priests who wandered round the great stone with prayers and flasks of holy water. 'Don't speak of the Devil. You may raise him up,' he warned.

The travelling barber-surgeon nodded wisely and tapped the side of his nose. 'You're right, friend. So what has happened to the stones?'

'The church has told us to bury them. That's what we've been doing for the past year. It's hard work in this cursed rain, though.'

'It can't have rained all year,' the traveller laughed.

The freeman didn't even smile. 'Seems like it. Seems every time we come near the stones a storm cloud can appear out of the clearest sky. I wish they were gone.'

The traveller shrugged. 'You have to do what the Church tells you. But tell me, friend, can I interest you in a pair of fine fat slimy leeches. Just three silver pennies?'

'I'd pay that much for you to take my place on this digging. I'm heart-sick of it.'

The traveller was a strong man and the work looked a simple way to make enough for a good meal and a few drinks at the tavern. The two men agreed and the freeman passed the spade to the traveller. 'What do I do?' the man asked, spitting on the palms of his hands.

'We dig a deep pit alongside each stone. When the pit's long enough we tunnel under the stone till it topples into the pit. Then we cover it over. We bury it.'

'It looks long enough now!' the traveller said.

'Aye. We're about to start digging away under the stone. Get yourself down there next to Peter the Ploughboy,' the freeman ordered.

The stranger slipped on the wet grass and slid quickly into the pit, splashing the workers with mud. They glared at him. He grinned back. 'The Devil's sent you lovely weather for this work!' he laughed.

The workers looked afraid and turned their backs on him. They began to dig the soil from under the looming stone. What happened next happened quickly. The dim light at the bottom of the trench was lit by a sudden flash. Moments later thunder rumbled and then teeming rain began to lash at the diggers.

The rain ran down the walls of the trench into a deep pool and crept over the tops of their boots. It also washed at the soil holding the mighty stone in place.

A panic gripped the men. They scrabbled for the leather ladder. Others reached up and clawed at the helping hands. The freeman reached down and held out a hand for the stranger. As their hands touched there was a gurgling and a groaning as the stone leaned towards the greasy jaws of the pit.

The freeman looked up and leaned back a little, making the traveller's mud-slimed fingers slip from his.

The man tumbled backwards and hit the pool of water hard. His cry was smothered when his head went under the water and by the rushing noise of the falling stone.

The stone fitted the pit perfectly. Brown mud oozed up its sides with perhaps a faint trace of red. The workers stepped forward and looked at the bubbling foam around its edges. The rain stopped as suddenly as it had begun.

'What do we do?' someone asked a priest. 'We'll never get him out of there.'

The pale priest whispered. 'No need. He has a bigger gravestone than any man in Avebury. Cover it up.'

'What about the other stones?' someone asked.

The priest looked around the grim slabs of stone and at the muddy mounds of the buried ones. 'They can stay,' he said sourly. 'We'll take this as a warning.'

Awesome Avebury

It was in 1938 that a man's skeleton was found at Avebury, crushed during the attempt to bury a stone in the 1320s. The man's neck was broken. His foot was trapped by the stone so his body couldn't be taken away. He had scissors and a razor in his pockets, so he was almost certainly a travelling surgeon who'd stopped on his travels to help out.

His purse still held three silver coins. The victim of an Avebury Temple curse?

He certainly didn't rest in peace after the archaeologists found him in 1938. His skeleton went to the College of

Surgeons in London to be examined. It was destroyed by a bomb during the Second World War.

To be crushed once is unlucky. To be crushed twice sounds like a curse!

After the 1320s Avebury accident there came the Black Death in 1349. There weren't enough healthy peasants to finish the work, even if they wanted to. The stones were safe ... for a while.

- In the 1600s and 1700s stones were broken up to make houses.
- Some were removed because the local council said they scared horses as it grew dark. (Maybe the horses could sense something their drivers couldn't!)

- In the 1800s some were moved to make farming easier.
- Even in 1976 the road ran so close to the ring that cars bumped it and a lorry knocked stone number 46 out of line.

STONE AGE SPOOKS

People are finding Stone Age objects all the time. It's not just professional archaeologists who dig them up but people on picnics, walkers in woods and maniacs with metal detectors.

Of course a lot of the people who go out looking for ancient relics aren't interested in history at all – they are interested in finding valuable things that they can sell. Buried treasure, in fact!

LOOK! IT'S AN EARLY TECHNOLOGY AGE BARTERING POUCH!

HE'S FOUND SOMEONE'S WALLET

But before you go ferreting in Farmer Fowl's fields for your fortune it is only fair to warn you ... there are *dangers*.

1 You need a landowner's permission to dig in a field or to walk on it looking for objects. If you don't have that, the landowner may simply shoot you with a shotgun. And shotgun pellets take a long, painful time to pick out from under the skin of your backside.

2 Amateurs without training can destroy more than they uncover. Best to join your local Young Archaeologists group – your local library should give you their address.

3 The ghosts of the Stone-Agers you disturb may come and get you.

Now you may think the third one there, the idea of Stone Age spooks, is just plain silly. But some people take them very seriously. And some people take them very, very, very, seriously...

Blood-chilling barrows

Stone-Agers were often buried in barrows. (No, dummy, that *doesn't* mean they were stuck in a *wheel*barrow instead of a coffin. 'Barrows' or 'cairns' are what archaeologists call the mounds where humans were buried.)

Barrows were built of earth, cairns of stone. The materials could be heaped over the corpses or there could be a stone or wooden room built and then covered over.

A barrow was just a little house for your putrefying pals. Some archaeologists reckon they were made to look like the Stone Age houses of the living – a sort of retirement hostel for the dead where they would feel at home.

Very cosy. There were different types of barrow and some have been given cute names by archaeologists...

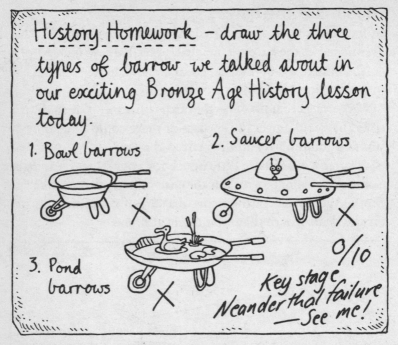

History Homework – draw the three types of barrow we talked about in our exciting Bronze Age History lesson today.

1. Bowl barrows

2. Saucer barrows

3. Pond barrows

0/10

Key stage Neanderthal failure —See me!

These barrows are found all over the world and were still being used by people like the Vikings up until the Middle Ages. The most common type of barrows built during the earlier Neolithic Age are 'Long' Barrows. They are called that because, believe it or not, they are *long*!

A good example is the Fussell's Lodge Barrow – an early English barrow. Archaeologists reckon it took at least ten people to build it. Fussell's Lodge is a log house over 100 metres long. The low wooden house was then buried under a *thousand* tonnes of chalk and soil.

The chalk was dug out of trenches at the side of the Lodge using only picks made of deer antlers. Digging must have been back-breaking work and carrying it over to the barrow must have been exhausting...

At one end of a long barrow there was usually a 'mortuary house'. That's where the dead body was left to rot till the flesh fell off and the bones could be scraped clean before they were buried. The barrows could be re-entered so people could perform rituals with the bones. Fussell's Lodge was used for hundreds of years then abandoned.

Then, in the later Neolithic and Bronze Age, the barrows changed to 'round' barrows. Bet you'll never guess what shape they were! Yes! They were triangular … no, only joking. They were shaped as a round dome – like a giant Christmas pudding that's trying to get in the *Guinness Book of Records*.

ROUND IS THE FASHIONABLE SHAPE FOR A MODERN CORPSE

Silly Hill 1

The strangest of these prehistoric monuments has to be Silbury Hill which was built around 2,700 BC. It's 40 metres high and is 160 metres across – so it's as wide as St Paul's Cathedral and a third of its height. It would have taken 700 men 10 years to build it. It needed more effort than Stonehenge and it's the greatest piece of prehistoric building in England.

In 1776 a group of miners dug a hole from the top to the bottom to find the secret of the hill. In 1849 a tunnel was dug through the side of the hill. In 1969 a television expedition recorded the digging of another tunnel.

What did they find?

a) the grave of a Stone Age chief – probably the first chief of Wiltshire

b) the treasure of the first Stone Age royal family – gold, silver and coins

c) the grave of a warrior, seated on his horse and covered in stone armour

d) a store of corn that was buried and never unearthed by the farmers

Answer: You are wrong! Whatever answer you chose is *wrong*. Because the answer is that the diggers found *nothing*. A big fat zippo, zilch and zippety plonk. Nil, naught and nix.

Modern humans like to think they're cleverer than Stone-Agers ... but they can't work out why Silbury Hill was built. But we know, don't we...

WORLD'S FIRST ARTIFICIAL SKI SLOPE! MORE FUN THAN THE PYRAMIDS OF EGYPT —AND MORE SNOW!

Silly Hill 2

There have been lots of legends that try to explain how Silbury hill got there. Many involve the Devil. One story says the Devil was planning to drop a vast shovel of earth on the town of Devizes. The townsfolk sent out a cobbler with a sack of old boots. He met the Devil, who was having a rest.

'How far is it to Devizes?' the Devil asked.

The cobbler tipped out the boots on to the ground. 'Well, I left Devizes three years ago and these are the boots I've worn out,' the cobbler explained.

The Devil groaned and said, 'Aw, Hell![1] I'm not walking all that way!' and he dumped the soil on the spot. That pile of soil is Silbury Hill.

It's good to know that someone as evil as the Devil is so thick! Anyone with any sense would have checked the map before he set out and seen that Devizes is just 8 miles away along the A361!

If you want to visit this useless lump of soil be warned! It is said to be haunted by the ghost of King Sil, who is buried there, in gold armour, astride his horse. (Except he *isn't* because archaeologists didn't find him when they dug through the soil. Of course, he may have just popped out for a ride.)

Golden ghosts

Many of the ancient tales about barrows seem to be about hidden treasures. *You* know that Stone-Agers didn't have gold (though some of the later barrow-builders did). *You* know that it's stupid to wreck an ancient barrow grave in a greedy search for golden gain. But that hasn't stopped

1. Don't worry ... this is *not* swearing. Hell is where the devil lives. So, when he says, 'Oh, Hell!' it's a bit like you saying, 'Oh! Home!' or, 'Oh, 25 Duckpool Terrace!'

devilish diggers delving down to the depths to find ... what?

In Cornwall a barrow was supposed to hold the ancient king of Cornwall in a golden boat with silver oars – grave plunderers found only a chest full of ashes. Other sites are said to hold cauldrons of gold, a golden calf (that's a popular one), a silver coffin, a man in golden armour on horseback, a golden chest, a golden table and even a golden wheelbarrow!

DO I GET A COFFIN OR A CAULDRON OR A CALF? NO. I GET A PIECE OF HANDY GARDENING EQUIPMENT!

It's true that there was an old legend of gold in Bryn yr Ellyhon (Goblin Hill) in Wales and in 1833 a golden cape *was* dug up. (The cape is now in the British Museum, so it's true.)

The horrible historical legend was that a ghost haunted the barrow at Goblin Hill and the ghost was dressed in gold; when the barrow was broken into, the gold cape was found. Does that prove the ghost story was true?

Strange, huh?

Almost as strange as the tale of a potty priest with a potion...

The huntsman's horror

Seriously spooky

The ghost stories that surround Stone Age sites may sound daft and doubtful to us. But the spirits of the dead Stone-Agers are causing *serious* problems for archaeologists today.

For hundreds of years people have been digging up these ancient bones and forgetting something very important: these bones once belonged to a living person.

Imagine your grave being dug up 5,000 years from now and your bones tested with radiocarbon dating. *You* would be upset at the thought.

Since the late 1970s some people have become just as upset. In Australia, the Aborigines are demanding that all the archaeological finds are returned to their holy grounds. In the USA, the Native Americans went even further, as a 1998 case shows...

The case of the missing bones

124

So? What would you say if you were the judge? Would you agree with the archaeologists that old bones can be dug up, examined and kept in a museum? If you say *that*, then how many unhappy spirits will be stirred up?

Or would you support the Native Americans and insist that they be given a proper burial? If you do, then the science of archaeology could end in 1998!

Not a very easy choice, is it?

Verdict: The judge declared the bones must be 'made available to science'. The archaeologists won the right to dig up and examine all the bones they want. When a ghost of the Ancient One appears at the foot of his bed the judge may regret that!

Nowadays, good archaeologists rebury the bones whenever it is possible.

EPILOGUE

People can't agree about what happened yesterday. When it comes to the truth about hominids who lived before writing was invented we have even less chance of agreeing.

Our understanding of prehistoric people changes with every new discovery; it changes every year ... every week! Ideas that were 'right' ten years ago are shown to be totally 'wrong' today ... and today's ideas will probably be proved wrong in another ten years.

So what is the very latest news on Stone-Agers? What is the hottest horrible history? It is this...

STONE AGERS WEREN'T AS HORRIBLE AS WE ONCE THOUGHT!

Stories of hideous hunters sucking brains out of fresh skulls may be wrong. And more. People may actually have been kind and thoughtful.

Here's a story about a Neanderthal with some clues about his life. You make up your own mind about the truth...

The man was quite old for a Neanderthal – around 40 years old in fact. He'd had a lot of bad luck and hardship in his life and, finally, he found himself in a cave when an earthquake shook the region. The cave roof cracked and collapsed on him. He was dead.

As a child he'd had a withered right arm that had never grown to full length or strength. The man had swollen joints (arthritis) and was blind in one eye. He'd been wounded on the skull but that had healed. Most gruesome of all he seems to have come off worst in a fight with a wild animal and damaged the end of his arm. One hand had been amputated by a sharp but crude stone knife.

His Neanderthal tribe would have been hunters who wandered the forests trapping and shooting animals or gathering fruits and nuts. This half-blind, limping, damaged man couldn't hold a bow and couldn't have been a lot of use to the others.

In Victorian times they might have shut him away in a hospital; in the Middle Ages they might have put him on display in a travelling fair; in Ancient Greece they may have left him in the hills to die in the jaws of a wolf.

But, in the Stone Age, this man *lived*.

Someone helped him, someone shared their hard-earned food, someone tended his wounds.

Someone *cared*.

The savage Stone Age?